TRACING
SCOTTISH
ANCESTORS

Rosemary Bigwood

HarperCollins

The verse on p.8 is an extact from *A Poem made when the Gaelic Society of Inverness was A Hundred Years Old* by Sorley MacLean, taken from *From Wood to Ridge: Collected Poems*, Carcanet Press 1989.

The illustration on p. 287 is based on one in J.H.S. Burleigh *A Church History of Scotland*, 1960)

HarperCollins Publishers
Westerhill Rd, Bishopbriggs, Glasgow G64 2QT

First published 1999

Updated edition 2001

www.**fire**and**water**.com

Reprint 10 9 8 7 6 5 4 3 2 1 0

© Rosemary Bigwood, 1999, 2001

ISBN 0 00 711102 9

Printed and bound in Great Britain by
Omnia Books Ltd, Glasgow G64

CONTENTS

List of Illustrations

*To my family
in thanks for their patience,
encouragement and enthusiasm.*

Smoke of the generations climbing
over peaks of memory of varying value,
the great men and the small
appearing and being lost in the hardship
that squinting fortune gives, or the choice
made by vision and devotion.

Sorley MacLean

1 PREPARATION

STARTING THE SEARCH

Embarking on research on family history is to start on a journey into the unknown, which may lead along many unexpected paths. This guide is planned as a practical aid to research – to help you find your way, to highlight some of the most important sources which you can use, to select those which are most likely to be relevant to your own research and to give guidance in understanding and interpreting what you discover.

Like all journeys, some pre-planning is important and you will find it rewarding to spend some time assessing what is already known about the family. One of Scotland's chief exports has been its people and therefore in many cases this initial work may take place outside Scotland, establishing the links which lead back to the generations born in that country.

Some people are only interested in finding the names of their ancestors and their dates of birth, death and marriage but most family historians want to put flesh on the bones, to know about the lives of those in earlier generations, where they lived and what they did. This guide, therefore, will include references to sources which will supply this information.

ORAL HISTORY & FAMILY TRADITIONS

Most families hand down stories about their past. An extraordinary number of people have been told that they are descended

---

CHECK YOUR FACTS

Memory is fallible, and any specific details as to dates, relationships or names of people which you are given must later be checked.

---

from Robert the Bruce, John Knox, Rob Roy McGregor or that one of their ancestors was the daughter of a titled family who ran away with the coachman and thereafter her name was erased from all the records. Such stories are unlikely to be true but should never be dismissed out of hand as there may be a grain of truth in them, though details may have been altered over the years.

Talking to older members of the family is always rewarding but is a matter which has to be handled with tact and care. Try to plan in advance what you want to know. History starts today and memories of what life was like fifty or more years ago can add an important dimension to a family history. Accounts of schooling, work conditions, home life, or war service will be valued by later generations. Keep full notes of all information you collect or use a tape recorder at the interview. In the Western Isles of Scotland, oral genealogies are still handed down from generation to generation – a most fruitful source of information.

PHOTOGRAPHS

Many families have collections of old photographs but often these present a problem as they are not annotated with names or dates. But you may be able to find some clues to aid in identification:

- Study the fashions of clothes worn – but bear in mind that in country districts and in the case of poorer families, people in the photographs may be not be wearing the newest fashions.

- See if there are any clues from the background such as cars, buildings or the studio setting for the photograph. There were various fashions for photographic studio settings which may indicate the date of taking the photograph. There are a number of books which will help – *Dating Old Photographs* by Robert Pols, *Photographs and Local History* by George Oliver and *Victorian Dress in Photographs* by Madeline Ginsburgh.

- Many family photographs were taken in studios by professional photographers. These will have the name of the studio and the name of the town either on the bottom of the picture or on the back. By checking a local trade directory (these exist for counties and many individual towns from the second half of the 19th century onwards and in some cases go back much earlier) it is often possible to identify the years when a particular photographer was working. This can provide an approximate dating for the photograph. *Scottish Trades, Professions, Vital Records and Directories – a Selected Bibliography* compiled by D.R. Torrance is a useful guide to directories.

FAMILY PAPERS & MEMORABILIA

- Old letters can be a source of enormous interest or of great frustration and, like photographs, may pose problems in identifying sender, recipient and persons mentioned (often referred to only by their initials or Christian names).

- Medals or inscribed presentations may lead to identification of service records or occupational information.

- Newspapers, with their accounts of weddings and funerals, and also of local and national events, are an excellent source of family history. A book of great value to family researchers is *Directory of Scottish Newspapers* compiled by Joan P.S. Ferguson which lists all Scottish newspapers, showing when they first appeared, when they ceased publication or amalgamated with others, and where copies of the papers can be consulted. Work is being carried out in various areas in indexing the local newspapers. To find out whether indexes have been made, contact the local librarian or archivist of the local authority archive (for addresses of the local authority archives see page 208).

- Family bibles are treasured possessions in some families, including details of births, deaths and marriages. Strangely enough, the details given are not always accurate – perhaps because they have in some cases been filled in after the event. Always take time to confirm the information written down there.

MONUMENTAL INSCRIPTIONS

Monumental inscriptions on gravestones can be the key to identifying several generations of a family and may include information crossing the ocean. Some tombstones for emigrant Scots in their new homes will detail where they came from or stones in Scotland may commemorate those who left the country. Many gravestones have become unreadable or have been destroyed and only a small proportion of people had a grave marked by a stone – but among those that have survived, people of all classes of society are represented. Bear in mind that people were not always buried in the place where they died: the family grave may be found in a burial ground in a different parish.

Work is in progress to record all surviving monumental inscriptions across Scotland and many of these records have been published by the Scottish Genealogy Society or by local family history societies. There is a very good collection at New Register House, Edinburgh, and the Scottish Genealogy Society (15 Victoria Terr., Edinburgh EH1 2JL) holds an even larger collection, including some which have not been published. Local family history societies, archives and libraries may also have additional records.

It is often difficult to read the old inscriptions and inevitably there are a number of mistakes in the published volumes, with wrong readings or omissions. For some burial grounds only the pre-1855 inscriptions have been recorded – which leaves a lot of valuable information untapped. Errors were also sometimes made in the inscriptions on the stones themselves – particularly with regard to ages. Whenever possible, go and study the actual stones. Take note whether there are stones of other people of the same surname near one in which you are interested. They may refer to previously unknown relatives. Unfortunately the stones in some burial grounds have been tidied up and moved.

Many of the late 17th-century and 18th-century stones are decorated with emblems indicating the craft or trade of the person buried there – the sextant of a mariner, cordiner's knife of a shoemaker, or agricultural tools of a farmer, for example. These may provide valuable clues as to the occupation of an ancestor. Betty Wilsher's book *Understanding Scottish Graveyards* has an excellent section on these symbols and other symbolic carvings.

SHARED INFORMATION

The coming of the Internet has made it possible for information on family history to be shared world-wide. There are an ever increasing – sometimes bewildering – number of web pages on genealogical subjects. These may cover lists of millions of names, articles which have been published, family trees which have been submitted, information about family and clan societies and holdings of archives and libraries. You can also send queries in the hope that someone will be able to answer your question.

The Scottish Genealogy Society has a *Register of Members' Interests* and it may be useful to check whether anyone else is researching the same family as yours. Many family history and clan societies also keep records of ongoing research and particular fields of interest. *The Genealogical Research Directory National and International*, edited by K.A. Johnson and Malcolm R. Sainty, is brought out annually, listing the names and addresses of persons all over the world who are interested in researching particular families at particular periods and places.

The Church of Jesus Christ of the Latter Day Saints (known as LDS or the Mormon Church) has compiled an *Ancestral File* of family information submitted by persons world-wide: this is available on CD disc and can be consulted at many family history centres. You may find a link with a line of your own family which has been researched but again a strong warning is necessary – the facts given may not be backed up by systematic research.

INTERNET WARNING

The information published on the Internet or sent to you in answer to particular queries may not be correct. The enthusiasm of surfers often outstrips their knowledge.

Do not jump to conclusions that because you share the same surname, you are related – or that your ancestors were related.

TRACING THE EMIGRANT ANCESTOR

For those who now live outside Scotland but are descendants of Scots emigrants, the problem is often to find that link back to the 'home' country. The *minimum* information needed to start research in Scotland is:

- a date or approximate date of a birth, death or marriage in Scotland after 1854 (when Statutory Registration was introduced) including enough information to prove that an entry is relevant – for example, names of parents of a child or an exact date and place of birth, the names of both spouses including the maiden name of the bride on a marriage, or age at death and place where it took place

  OR

- information as to where an individual was living in Scotland between 1841 and 1901 (the 1901 census is open in 2002). If the place of residence was one of the big cities, then an address must be known before you can tackle the mainly unindexed 1841-1871 censuses. Again, enough detail must be given to allow you to identify a relevant person. To know that John McLean or Mary Wilson lived in Paisley in 1861 is not sufficient to identify the right person. If, however, you know that John McLean and Mary Wilson married in Scotland and had a child named Charlotte born about 1854 and were living in Paisley in 1861, then even if the marriage and birth of the child were not registered, given patience and time, you could do the long search through the Paisley census and identify the right family.

OR

- if the family left Scotland before 1855, details (backed up by sufficient means of identification of a relevant entry) of a birth (or baptism) or marriage in Scotland. Death and burial records before 1855 are few and far between.

Finding the Links

Every country where the emigrant Scot settled has its own kinds of records and the following are some general suggestions on steps to take in looking for those vital clues leading back to Scotland:

- Establish who was the emigrant ancestor and, if possible, the approximate date when he or she left Scotland. The date may sometimes indicate the circumstances under which the person emigrated and lead to records giving personal details. For example, prisoners were sent out to America after the 1715 and 1745 Jacobite rebellions – and at earlier times: convicts were transported to Australia between 1788 and 1868: a number of disbanded soldiers settled in America after the end of the Seven Years War (1756–63). These facts may lead back to court records or army or other records which include further clues.

- Consider why the person emigrated from Scotland and what was his or her occupation. Often groups of people left Scotland together and there may be records dealing with their emigration. The flow of Highlanders out of Scotland at the end of the 18th and early 19th centuries was often the result of a particular landlord clearing his lands of the tenants. Information about some members of the group may provide clues about others. Find out as much as you can about the status of the new immigrant.

- See whether there is a relevant passenger list. This was usually kept at the port of disembarkation – if it has survived, and too few have. A great deal of work is in progress on indexing passenger lists. Remember that Scottish emigrants may have sailed from England or Ireland, having first journeyed there from their homes. There are very few passenger lists in Scotland.

- Look for immigration records, naturalisation papers, marriage or death certificates in the country where the immigrant settled. These may give some vital information – names of parents, place of birth and age.

- Newspaper obituaries often include details of the background of the deceased and include information on Scottish origins.

- Take note of all family traditions and stories, looking for clues.

- Contact other branches of the family and see if they have any additional information and check whether their traditions and family details agree with yours.

- Consider the possibility that the surname may have been changed slightly when the family settled in their new home. If the immigrant was illiterate, officials often had to take down unfamiliar names as they heard them.

- Check the Christian names of children born to an emigrant Scot: a middle name was often the maiden name of the mother or another relative. Family naming traditions may still continue.

- Search for wills or other legal documents to see if reference is made to a relative back in Scotland.

- Emigrants who bought land in their new country sometimes named the property after the place where they lived in Scotland. This often happened in Australia.

- Try to find your immigrant ancestor in a census in his or her new country. Entries can be frustrating in only giving 'Scotland' as place of birth but all information may be welcome. The availability of census returns in other countries varies widely.
  England – census returns (as in Scotland) taken decennially and open for research from 1841-1901 (there is a 100 years' closure on access). The earlier census returns, 1801-1831, were collected to produce official returns, published as Parliamentary Papers, though some of the parish overseers did take nominal listings in the process of making up their official return and in some places these are kept in local record offices.
  Ireland – very few returns have survived before the census of 1901 – the first extant complete census. Full details of Irish census returns are given in *Tracing Irish Ancestors*.
  USA – censuses for some states go back to 1790. *Census Index Availability Guide* by Andrew J Morris details what has survived.
  Canada – the earliest census returns go back to the late 17th century, and cover some French settlements. Records for other parts of the country vary greatly. Ontario and Quebec are covered by decennial returns from 1851 onwards and there are indexes to later returns for various other parts of Canada.
  Australia – very few census returns exist, though the 1828 New South Wales census is published and indexed. There are a few population surveys known as Musters from 1788: some are only concerned with convicts.

GETTING PROFESSIONAL HELP

One of the frustrations of family history research is that you may not be able to do it all yourself. Hiring a professional genealogist is not cheap but in the end of the day it may save you money – and trouble. Genealogical magazines and websites include many advertisements for researchers – offering friendly, professional, reliable or efficient service – but it is not easy for the uninitiated to separate out the cowboys from the real professionals.

The Association of Scottish Genealogists and Record Agents (known as ASGRA) was founded in 1981 and membership is open to experienced and well-qualified professional searchers who sign a Code of Practice. Members have had a wide training and considerable experience and any complaints about their work can be referred to the Association. A list of members can be obtained from ASGRA, 51/3 Mortonhall Road, Edinburgh EH9 2HN (website http://www.asgra.co.uk). The ASGRA leaflet states the recommended basic hourly rate for carrying out research. Most genealogists in Scotland (unlike those in England and some other places) work both as record agents, looking for a particular piece of information, and as genealogists who will undertake the oversight of a complete family history. Look carefully at the description given on any leaflet or advertisement for the kind of work undertaken by the researcher and check whether you think it suits the kind of research you require. Some are experts in particular fields, have special interests, will research in particular archives or libraries and state that they can read Latin or Old Scots handwriting – necessities in older research.

When contacting a researcher, take care in making your

research request. State clearly what you already know (and whether it is proven) and what you want to know. Some researchers will ask for fees in advance, others are trusting and do the work first, but in either case it is wise to agree on a budget in hours or to decide on a certain sum of money to be spent on research. Once you have corresponded with the researcher, he or she will be able to advise you on this. If the project is a large one, you may want to have the work done in instalments. It is rarely possible for a researcher to estimate in advance how long a particular search will take. This will depend on the complexity of the case and the kind of records which have to be consulted. Remember that a search *may* result in a lot of negative findings: panning for genealogical gold can be a chancy business.

The Scottish Genealogy Society, Scottish family history societies and local authority archivists may answer simple queries, but do not expect this advice to be free. The National Archives of Scotland will answer postal enquiries and give advice on source material but they cannot carry out lengthy genealogical research. Some family history societies have lists of local researchers.

RECORDING RESEARCH

Get organised from the start. It is too easy to start jotting down notes on odd bits of paper or to think 'Of course, I will remember that'. Ideally you need to record your research in such a way that someone else can pick up your notes and find them intelligible!

Record keeping is a matter of personal preference. Loose-leaf notebooks or card indexes are preferred by some but increasingly, records are kept on the computer. Some people like to enter findings on Family Group sheets of various kinds but unless you are only interested in the 'skeleton' of your family and the names and dates of each generation, make sure that you have enough space to add notes. It is a fault of many genealogy programs that there is insufficient scope for adding in general information. However you organise your work – by generation, by individual or by family – make sure that you can find your own way through your notes, can add to them, rearrange them and refer to them quickly and easily.

Always have on hand a chart for easy visual reference. This may be a drop-line chart which includes all the members of each generation of a family; this is very useful but often difficult to organise when families are large and you have traced back a number of generations. Pedigree charts are simpler but only record the name

---

KEEPING RECORDS

- Always note the full reference for your source material (name of book, author, page number, document reference and where the book or document was found).

- Note when the book or document was written and whether it was contemporary to the event.

- Note the period of years over which the source material (such as parish registers) was searched.

- Note negative as well as positive findings so that you do not have to duplicate research.

- Note the characteristics of manuscript material – such as gaps in registers, evidence that they were not well kept, illegible writing – or any known bias of the writer.

---

of the main-line ancestor (not the siblings) in each generation with dates and places of birth, death and marriage. Many computer genealogy programs include these charts which you can fill in.

Scottish Family History by Margaret Stuart has an introduction which is an excellent and practical guide to the different ways of writing a family history.

WORKING FROM HOME

Once you have carried out the preliminaries in sorting out what you know about a person or family and what you want to find out, you may have opportunities to do some initial research quite close to home. If you live in the district from which your ancestors originated, explore the facilities of your local libraries, nearest family history society and local authority archive. These may have a great deal of local material of value, including microfilm copies of parish registers of the locality and perhaps of the census returns.

LDS Records

Find out where your nearest Latter Day Saints library is. There are LDS family history centres throughout the world and through them you will be able to order microfilm copies of any of the wide range of records held in the LDS library in Salt Lake City. Some libraries have built up their own holdings of microfilmed copies of records. All these libraries will have a copy of the *Family History Library Catalogue* from which you can select what you need. It may take some weeks for your reel of film to arrive – and there is a charge for getting it.

> The LDS programme of filming records has made a wide range of material available to family historians round the world but remember that there is a wealth of Scottish material which is **not** in the LDS library. Reference will be made to these sources in later chapters of this book.

FAMILY SEARCH

Family Search on CD-ROM is a world-wide searching aid compiled by the LDS. It has a section on the British Isles, which can then be narrowed down to Scotland. It can be consulted in LDS libraries and also in some other family history centres – and in New Register House. The *Family History Library Catalogue* for Salt Lake City is on disc and there is also a section called *Ancestral File*. This is a computerised collection of genealogies, which links families into pedigrees. The information has been contributed by individuals, families and genealogical organisations round the world and there is an ongoing programme of additions and corrections. It may be useful to consult this source but it is important to remember that the information supplied for these pedigrees is only vouched for by the contributor.

SCOTTISH CHURCH RECORDS

This is another section of *Family Search*. It includes most of the Indexes to baptisms and marriages recorded in the Old Parish Registers but does include a few extra entries taken from non-Church of Scotland registers.

THE INTERNATIONAL GENEALOGICAL INDEX

These LDS libraries will hold copies of the International Genealogical Index (known as the IGI) and it can also be consulted in many other archives and family history centres. The IGI is an index of baptisms and marriages (indexed together) in countries round the world. It is arranged on a country basis. Various editions have appeared, the early (microfiche) ones for Scotland (before 1984) including baptisms and marriages in one undivided index for the whole country, the later editions being divided into county sections. The 1992 index is available on microfiche and the 1993 index on CD-ROM – in a set covering the British Isles, which forms part of *Family Search*.

Information on the IGI is taken from two sources: records compiled by individuals who have submitted the results of their genealogical research for Temple ordinance information; and the LDS library's programme of systematic extraction of various records. In Scotland these include the greater part of the index to the old parish registers and most of the indexes to the statutory registers of birth and marriage 1855–75. Each new edition of the IGI has new entries added to it but at the same time – particularly in the latest edition – some names are removed from the index.

The IGI is a very useful searching tool but it should be used with great care. By searching the Index on CD-ROM, it is possible to search the Index for the whole of Scotland for one particular entry or to collect together – over a given period – all children born to a named couple.

The advantage of the Index is that it includes some baptisms of children in non-Church of Scotland congregations: the disadvantage is that some of the information is incorrect, there are omissions and corroboration of the accuracy or existence of a particular entry cannot always be found.

Scots Origins – Database to GRO indexes

This is an online pay-per-view database of indexes to the genealogical records of the General Register Office in New Register House, Edinburgh. It includes:

- Indexes of the statutory registers of births and marriages from 1855 to 1898 (this will be adapted annually to give a 100-year closure), and of deaths to 1917
- Indexes to births/baptisms and proclamations/marriages in all the Old Parish Registers
- Indexes to the 1891 census for the whole of Scotland.

The GRO website is http://www.origins.net. On payment of a fee (at present £6) you will be given 30 page credits, each page consisting of a maximum of 15 search results. If from the index entry you see a reference to an entry for which you would like the certificate, you can order it direct from the database to be sent to you by post at a present cost of £10 per certificate. The advantage of this is that you may be able to do some work on the indexes at home – but you must never rely on these alone.

In some family history centres direct links have now been made with the New Register House computer indexes to the statutory registers, Old Parish Registers and the 1881 and 1891 censuses for the whole of Scotland and on payment of a fee you can access all these indexes.

2 SCOTTISH NAMES

SURNAMES

The computerisation of indexes has brought many benefits but it has also brought some problems in its wake. The computer will only answer to the information which you key in and as a result of spelling variants of names and changes of names, you may find your search results in a dead end.

Spelling in the past was often very idiosyncratic. Many people had little education or were illiterate. This might result in problems. Perhaps, for example, a registrar in the Lowlands had to record the birth of the child of a Gaelic-speaking incomer from the Highlands who was difficult to understand. The registrar then had to write down the name as he heard it. Another registrar in a neighbouring district might represent the name differently.

It may help to consider the following points:

- Try to think of possible variant spellings of a surname. The computers in New Register House have a facility for keying in 'similar-sounding names' which is good but does not cover all name variants (and includes many which are not variants). It is necessary to use this key to bring up surnames with the prefix 'Mc' or 'Mac' which are completely interchangeable but are indexed separately in the computer indexing system.

- It may sometimes help to look at the International Genealogical Index for a particular area in which you are interested. Births and marriages are entered in the IGI with the original spelling of the entry but are grouped according to a standardised form of the name. You can therefore *see* a range of the variants of that surname and program your computer accordingly.

- In early times Qu might be used for Wh and therefore the surname Whitelaw/Whytelaw might appear as Quhytelaw.

- Many Highland names changed about the end of the 18th century or later. Sometimes the prefix O' or Mc/Mac was dropped. Names starting with 'McGille' were often shortened to 'McIl'. Some surnames were anglicised: Henderson and Hendry are found earlier as McKendrick; Keith was a later form of McKichan or McKeich; Pursell was a 'translation' of McSporran. *The Surnames of Scotland* by George F Black lists most Scottish surnames and gives examples of name changes as well as of alternative spellings and forms.

- In Gaelic-speaking areas, patronymics may be found in earlier records showing the ancestral links through several generations, using the genitive case of 'Mc' – 'Vic' or Vc' – as in the name Donald MacCoil vic Ean vic Coil. Sometimes two surnames are linked by an alias – often a family name added to a clan name.

- In some non-Gaelic areas and in the north of Scotland – particularly in Shetland – patronymics were used by some families till the 19th century or even later. The son was known by his father's Christian name: thus Gilbert Johnson might be the son of John Williamson, while Gilbert's son, James, would be known as James Gilbertson.

- Differentiation of individuals within communities where one or two surnames were common, was often made by adding descriptive epithets – mhor (big), beg (little), dubh (black), ban (fair), for example or by the use of nicknames.

- Women may continue to be known by their maiden names even when married or widows.

CHRISTIAN NAMES

Spelling and variant forms of Christian names can also cause trouble. Elizabeth/Elisabeth are interchangeable and you may find Catherine also spelt Catharine, Katherine/Katharine or Cathrine/Kathrin/Kathren. Janet often appears as Jonet in older records. You may sometimes be well advised not to key in a Christian name when using the computer indexes – or to use an initial alone.

The following are some of the alternative forms of Scottish christian names which you may find:

Agnes, Nancy
Angus, Aeneas and Aonghas
Christian, Christina and Kirsty
Donald and Daniel
Helen, Ellen, Nelly
Hugh, Hew, Ewan and Aodh
Isabella (Isabel/Isobel/Isobella), Bella, Elizabeth, Betty and
    Beatrice/Beatrix
Jane, Janet, Jean, Jessie
John, Iain, Eun/Eoin
Margaret, Maggie and Peggy
Morah/Morag and Sara(h)
Peter and Patrick
Samuel and Sorley

Many Scots Christian names end in 'ina' – Robertina, Donaldina or Williamina. These are often shortened to Ina. In registers, Christian names may be abbreviated – Wm for William, Rot. for Robert, Jas. for James and Margt. for Margaret – and therefore if you key in William McLean on your computer, you will not find Wm McLean coming up on the screen. To be safe, just key in 'W. McLean', remembering that you will also have to press the 'similar sounding names' key to cover MacLean.

PLACE-NAMES

All the warnings about spelling of surnames apply to the recording of place-names. It may be helpful to say aloud a written name, when you will realise what is the modern form.

COMMON PLACE-NAMES

There are a great many places with the same name in many different parts of the country. If, for example, you have an ancestor born in Kilmichael, Newton or Ballimore, you will need to discover in which part of the country this place was situated. There is a parish of Leslie in Fife and another of the same name in Aberdeenshire: there is a Pathhead in Midlothian, another in Fife and yet another in Ayrshire. Do not jump to conclusions as to the geographic location of the place unless you have proof.

3 CIVIL REGISTRATION – BIRTHS, MARRIAGES & DEATHS

NEW REGISTER HOUSE – RECORD HOLDINGS

Once you have decided on the starting point for research on your family history, if this is after 1854, you may need to visit the General Register Office for Scotland at New Register House or instruct someone to do this for you.

New Register House is a treasure store of genealogical material. It holds three main series of records:

- Statutory civil registers from 1 January 1855 onwards

- Decennial census returns which are open for consultation from 1841–1901 – the 1901 census will be accessible in 2002

- Old Parish Registers for the whole of Scotland.

There are also various minor records:

- Register of divorces from May 1984

- Marine births and deaths from 1855 and Air register from 1948

- Army returns of births, deaths and marriages 1881–1959 abroad and Service Department Registers from 1959 outwith the UK

- War Registers from 1899: South African War deaths of Scottish soldiers 1899-1902; World War I (Scottish soldiers but not

officers); Scottish naval Petty Officers and men; World War II
(incomplete returns)

- Consular returns of births, deaths and marriages from 1914
- High Commissioners' returns of births and deaths from 1964
- Register of births, deaths and marriages in foreign countries
  1860–1965
- Foreign marriages from 1947

The minor records are indexed and entries have been included in
the relevant computerised indexes – of birth, death or marriage –
of the statutory registers.

RESEARCHING AT NEW REGISTER HOUSE

New Register House is at the east end of Princes Street (near
Waverley Station, opposite the Balmoral Hotel) and is open from
9.00 to 16.30 Monday to Friday (except some public or local holidays). You cannot park there and do not bring luggage as there
are no storage facilities. Special arrangements can be made for dis-
abled persons. There are over a hundred seats available but sometimes the search rooms are full and if you are coming from a distance, it may be wise to book a seat in advance; telephone 0131
314 4433. Your place will then be held till 10.00 on that day.

On arrival you will have to buy a pass for access to the records
– *including to the indexes*. A pass can be bought which is valid for
a day (at present £17), a week (£65), four weeks (£220), a quarter
(£500) – or for a year (£1500). You can also purchase a pass for a
half-day search (available after 13.00 only on the day) if space is
available (£10). If you want to spend a week in New Register

STATUTORY REGISTRATION

Statutory registration was introduced in Scotland in January 1855. From that date onwards, district registrars have recorded all births, marriages and deaths and have forwarded copies of these certificates to the General Register Office for Scotland at New Register House in Edinburgh. Annual indexes to each group of records are then compiled for the whole of Scotland and are now available on computer.

Certificates can be consulted at the local registrar's office on payment of a fee (telephone in advance to find whether this is possible) but you will almost certainly find it more rewarding to go New Register House where you can consult certificates registered everywhere in Scotland.

In Scotland, access is presently allowed not only to the indexes of the statutory certificates but also to the actual certificates. This means that a great deal can be achieved in even one day's searching as there is no limit – while your time and energy last – to the number of certificates you can check.

House, it is a good idea to try to arrange a visit on two days at the end of one week and three at the beginning of the next. A week's pass is valid for five consecutive days' searching. You may think that the pass is expensive but you will find it gives you access to an enormous range of source material and that you can get a great deal done in a day. Payment for your pass can be made by Switch, Visa or MasterCard or by a sterling cheque backed by a British cheque card. (Prices may vary from year to year.)

You will be shown to a desk in one of the search rooms which will have on it a computer terminal and a fiche-reading machine. There are microfilm readers nearby for use by all pass holders.

Most records are on fiche or microfilm and there is self-service access – a member of staff will explain the system to you and show you where to find the records. You can collect three fiches at a time or two microfilms. Fill out the relevant order slip (for statutory certificate, census or Old Parish Register) and leave it in the cabinet drawer in the place from which you took out the fiche or film. Once you have finished with the fiche or microfilm, replace it in the designated box in the search room and the repository assistants will put it away.

You can use a laptop computer but there are no mains supplies. All work must be done in pencil. You may find it useful to bring prepared forms on which to record the information you find on certificates or on census returns as it is very easy to get carried away by enthusiasm and to forget to record some of the vital details. Forms are on sale at New Register House.

If you have a pass of any kind, you can order personally a certified copy of any statutory certificate, census entry or parish register entry for £8 (if you order this by post it will cost you £13). For statutory certificates which are more than one hundred years old, you can order up an uncertified copy for £2.50 (not available for census returns or OPR entries). These certificates cannot be used for legal purposes and the quoted charges may change.

INDEXES TO THE STATUTORY REGISTERS

Birth Indexes

Key into your computer terminal the year when you think the child was born, male or female, the surname and the Christian

Keep a note of the number of the entry you want to see. Each fiche contains copies of nearly a hundred certificates and you must know which one to consult.

name or an initial. A list of entries will then come up on the screen showing the surname and Christian name of the child, the name of the district in which the birth certificate was registered, the number given to that district and the number of the entry in the particular book. The number of entries which appear on the screen may be daunting if the surname is a common one but the fact that the name of the registration district is given may help if you know in which part of the country the family were likely to have been living.

Select the entry or entries which may be relevant and fill in the order slip on your desk, with your name, seat number, date, the year of the entry, number of the registration district (you do not need to put down its name) and number of the entry.

If you do not think any of the entries on your screen is the cor-

BIRTH INDEX SHORT-CUT

Most (but not all) births and marriages registered between 1855 and 1875 are included in the 1992 and other editions of the IGI. The IGI Index gives the name of the registration district where the child was born, the date of birth and most importantly – the names of the parents. If you know the names of the child's parents, you can see at a glance whether an index entry is relevant or not and avoid the necessity of consulting a number of certificates to find the right one.

rect one, you can press keys to pass on to the next year or to the previous one. Unfortunately, between 1855 and 1928 the indexes provide no clue as to the parentage of the child: from 1929 onwards the maiden name of the child's mother is given in the index which makes it much easier to decide whether the entry is the one you wanted.

If you think the surname might be spelt in a number of ways (and remember that Mc – and Mac – are regarded as two separate names), then use the key on your computer to bring up 'similar sounding surnames'.

Having written out your requisition slip, take it to the nearest cabinets containing the fiche copies of the certificates. The fiches are arranged by years and by district number, with separate cabinets for births, marriages and deaths.

Marriage Indexes

As for births, key in the year, sex, Christian name and surname of the person whose marriage you are seeking. If you know the name of both bride and bridegroom, there is a facility on the computer for entering both surnames (with or without Christian names). This cross-referencing makes it much easier to find the right entry, though unfortunately if the surname of the bride and bridegroom

---

MARRIAGE INDEX SHORT-CUT

If either the bride or bridegroom has an unusual Christian name or surname, it may be quicker to key in that name alone, rather than using the cross-referencing facility.

---

is the same you cannot use the cross-referencing facility. Again, bear in mind possible spelling alternatives of one or both names. You can work through a series of years quite quickly just by altering the year – you do not need to type in the whole entry each time. As with births, take down the year, district number and entry number on your slip and collect the fiche containing that entry.

Death Indexes

An entry in the Death Index will show you the sex, Christian name and surname of the person, as well as the registration district name, number and entry number. From 1974 onwards, the index includes the maiden name of the deceased's mother – useful in picking out the right entry. A woman is indexed at death under both her maiden and married name and you can cross-reference these names on the computer. If a woman married more than once, she should be indexed under her maiden name and both or all her married names but this does not always happen.

In 1855 and after 1865 the age at death is given but for the years 1856–65 this information is still rather sporadic though it is gradually being added to the Index. You can program the computer to select only entries between certain age limits. It is very important to remember that ages are frequently stated inaccurately and therefore you should cater for quite a big margin of error when searching for relevant death certificates. Make sure that the age parameters set on your computer are correct – they will appear in the top right-hand corner of the screen. If the numbers are 0-0, (and sometimes the computer defaults to this) you will only get entries of children who died under the age of one.

DEATH INDEX SHORT-CUT

If you are looking for the death of a husband and wife, look first for the death of the wife as you can cross-reference her maiden and married names on the computer. Her death certificate will tell you whether she was married or a widow when she died, and so you know whether to look for her husband's death either after or before this time.

Finding the Place

An index search may be complicated by not knowing where the registration districts are in Scotland. You may think that the person you are trying to trace was born in Ayrshire c. 1878 but unless you have a good geographical knowledge of the area, it is very difficult to pick out the registration districts which might be relevant to your search. The matter may be further complicated by the fact that Scotland's local government has been reorganised several times in recent years and counties – which were the unit of government till 1974 – no longer exist. The Parish Index at the end of this book will be of assistance in giving the parish number (which until recent times was in most places also the registration district number) and showing the county in which each parish was situated. It may also help to have at hand two publications that you can buy in New Register House. The first is the *Civil Parish Map Index,* a diagrammatic map of the parishes of Scotland, and the other is *Registration Districts of Scotland from 1855*, a book showing in which county or burgh each registration district is situated – and the reference number given to that district.

The registration districts of Scotland are numbered from the Shetland Islands downwards. Thus the parish of Bressay in Shetland is District Number 1, while Wigtown in the far south-west is number 901. Cities such as Aberdeen, Edinburgh, Dundee and Glasgow are divided into a number of districts, each having the same first number with a differentiating superscript number for the district within the city. These city divisions changed from time to time as the population expanded and in recent times certain registration districts have been renumbered.

Other useful searching aids are the various editions of the *Index of Scottish Place Names* published by HM Stationery Office which list the inhabited places in Scotland named in the various census returns and show the parish and county in which each was situated.

The *Ordnance Gazetteer of Scotland* by Francis H. Groome, of which various editions were published in the last decades of the 19th century, is often helpful, particularly in identifying the locality of small villages and towns which were not parishes. There are copies of this work in the search rooms of New Register House and it is widely available in libraries.

If your family remained in the same part of Scotland for some time – and many unfortunately did not – take some time to familiarise yourself with the geographical area by looking at maps. Further advice and information on maps is given on page 164.

INFORMATION IN STATUTORY CERTIFICATES

In Scotland, on purchase of a pass to New Register House, access is granted to the certificates (in England the indexes can be searched without charge but certificates must be ordered and payment made for each one). This makes it possible to determine immediately whether the entry selected in the indexes is the right one and is an enormous advantage.

Take down all the information. Scottish certificates include a great deal of detail which is most valuable when researching ancestry. On certificates registered in 1855 – the first year of statutory registration – more detail was included than in any other year. The following is a summary of what you will find on statutory certificates.

Birth Certificates

A birth certificate includes:

- The child's name; the date, time and place of birth
- The names of the parents including the maiden name of the mother and occupation of the father
- The date and place of the parents' marriage (**not** given on certificates between 1856 and 1860)
- The name of the informant on the birth – usually one of the parents but occasionally another relative – and details of the relationship of the informant to the child. If the informant was illiterate, he or she will sign with a cross.
- In 1855 certificates, details are also given of the ages of both parents, the place of birth of each and the number of children born to them (but not their names) – stating their sex and how many are still alive.

If a certificate is stamped on the side 'RCE' with a volume number

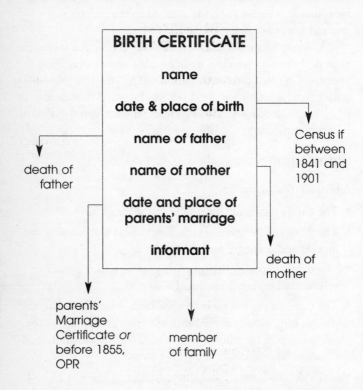

Birth Certificate – Where Next?

Opposite: **Marriage Certificate – Where Next?**

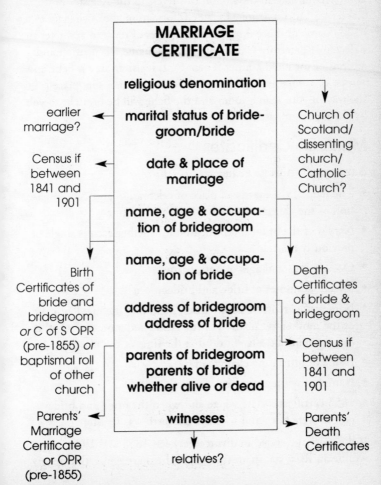

MARRIAGE CERTIFICATE

religious denomination → Church of Scotland/ dissenting church/ Catholic Church?

marital status of bride-groom/bride → earlier marriage?

date & place of marriage → Census if between 1841 and 1901

name, age & occupation of bridegroom

name, age & occupation of bride

Birth Certificates of bride and bridegroom *or* C of S OPR (pre-1855) *or* baptismal roll of other church

address of bridegroom address of bride → Death Certificates of bride & bridegroom

parents of bridegroom parents of bride whether alive or dead → Census if between 1841 and 1901

Parents' Marriage Certificate *or* OPR (pre-1855)

witnesses → Parents' Death Certificates

relatives?

41

and page number in the stamp, this refers to the Register of Corrected Entries. It may include information about changes to a child's name or more importantly, in cases of illegitimacy, refer to a decree of paternity which will state the name, occupation and address of the child's father. These RCE registers are on fiche and can be consulted in New Register House. Fill in a slip, place it in the tray in your search room and the fiche will be brought to you by the repository assistant.

Marriage Certificates

A marriage certificate includes:

- The date of the marriage, place of celebration and denomination of the church or whether before a registrar
- Names of the bride and bridegroom, whether each is single or previously married
- Occupations and ages of both parties
- Present addresses of bride and bridegroom
- Names of parents of both parties, including the maiden name of the mother, occupation of the father and a note of whether these parents are alive or dead at the time of the marriage
- Name of officiating clergyman
- Names of witnesses (often relatives)
- 1855 certificates state where and when the bride and bridegroom were born and whether the birth was registered.

If the marriage ended in divorce between 1855 and 1984, there will be an RCE stamp on the side of the marriage certificate, giving a volume and page number. From 1984 onwards there is a separate Register of Divorces granted by Scottish courts which shows the names of the parties, date and place of marriage, date and place of divorce and details of court orders regarding provision for the children.

Death Certificates

A death certificate includes:

- The name or names of the deceased person
- Occupation, marital status and the name of the spouse (if any) except between 1856 and 1860 when it is only noted whether the deceased was single, married, widow or widower, omitting the name of the spouse
- Date, time and place of death and note of usual address if this is not the place of death
- Parents' names, including maiden name of the mother, father's occupation and whether parent(s) are still alive
- Cause of death
- The name of the informant and relationship to the deceased – and sometimes the address of the informant
- Place of burial and name of the undertaker on certificates 1856–60 only
- 1855 death certificates also give of names of any issue of the deceased, with their ages at that time (1855) or ages at death if this had occurred earlier.

If there was an inquest following the death, then there will be an

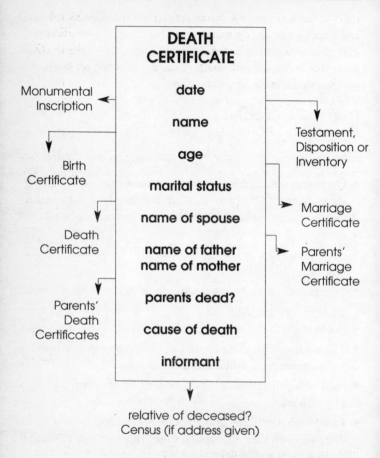

DEATH CERTIFICATE

date

Monumental Inscription ←

name

→ Testament, Disposition or Inventory

age

Birth Certificate

marital status

name of spouse

→ Marriage Certificate

Death Certificate

name of father
name of mother

→ Parents' Marriage Certificate

Parents' Death Certificates

parents dead?

cause of death

informant

relative of deceased?
Census (if address given)

Death Certificate – Where Next?

44

entry in the Register of Corrected Entries – the relevant volume and page number being stamped on the side of the certificate.

If you cannot read the fiche copy of a certificate, take the fiche to the supervisor of your search room and ask whether you can see the original copy of the certificate in the registration book. The book will then be brought to you within a short time.

Research Example

Always search systematically backwards when you are tracing your family tree. In this way you can be sure you have found the right entry.

If you start with a birth certificate, follow the steps given in this example:

Step 1 You have the birth certificate of George Reid born in 1927 and this will tell you that his parents were Hugh Reid and Maggie Skene who were married in 1926 in Banff.

Step 2 Consult the marriage certificate of Hugh Reid and Maggie (her name on the certificate could be Margaret) Skene. You then know that the names of the parents of Hugh Reid are John Reid and Williamina Cumming, that they were still alive when their son got married and how old Hugh was at the time of his marriage.

Step 3 Hugh said he was 25 when he married. Search the Indexes to Births circa 1901. You may have to follow up several index entries for the birth of a Hugh Reid between 1900 and 1902 as his year of birth would depend on the month in which he was born and the month when he married – but you will be able to

identify the right certificate as you know the names of his parents.
Step 4 The birth certificate will tell you when and where his parents, John Reid and Williamina Cumming, were married and so you can then find that marriage certificate.

Step 5 Next, you can either search for the death certificates of John Reid and his wife (after 1926 since they were still alive when their son was married) and these will name their parents and give age at death *or* go from the marriage certificate of John Reid and Williamina Cumming back to John Reid's birth certificate.

The system is the same whether you start from a birth, marriage or death certificate.

PROBLEM SOLVING

By searching back in this way, in most cases you can trace a family back to the beginning of the 19th century – sometimes a little earlier. A death certificate registered in 1861, for example, may state that the deceased was aged 70 and will name his parents. This provides the necessary detail to identify a relevant entry in the parish registers (if it has been recorded) circa 1791. There can, however, be problems. Particularly when you are dealing with a common surname, the sought-after person can get lost. Consider the following clues and possibilities of error.

1855 BIRTH, DEATH AND MARRIAGE CERTIFICATES

If you think that any member of your family – not just the main line ancestor – was born, married or died in 1855, check this certificate as it will contain a great deal of additional information.

RESEARCH TECHNIQUES IN NEW REGISTER HOUSE

Indexes are sometimes necessary, always useful, but you should never let them induce 'tunnel vision'. **Never rely on the indexes – always check the actual certificates.**

Take down **all** the information given on the certificate. The diagrams on pages 40, 41 and 44 will provide you with a check-list of information given on a certificate, reminding you of the clues which you can follow up.

- A middle name, assumed later in life, may not be given on the birth certificate.
- The year of birth – calculated from a marriage or death certificate – may be wrong. Search before and after the expected date.
- Births (marriages and deaths) occurring at the end of December may not be registered till January in the following year.
- If you have problems finding a birth, look first for the marriage of the parents (cross-referencing their names on the computer) which will act as a guide as to where the family were living.
- Occasionally when the mother of a child died soon after his/her birth, and the father remarried, the name of the second wife is given as the mother on the marriage or death certificate of that child.
- If you know that the ancestor had a brother or sister with an uncommon Christian name, look for that birth to gain information about where the family were living and when and where the parents married.

Births

- The child might have been born before the parents' marriage and have been recorded under the mother's maiden name.
- If the birth took place between 1855 and 1875, check the IGI of the county where you think the family lived. The IGI index includes the names of the child's parents but bear in mind that some statutory certificates within this period are not indexed on the IGI. You may be able to pick out other siblings of the main line ancestor.

Marriages

- The date and place of marriage given on birth certificates in 1855 and after 1860 may be inaccurate. If you do not find an entry in the expected year, search either side of that time. Remember that often the first child was born either before or very shortly after marriage.
- If the main line ancestor was born between 1856 and 1860, the birth certificate will not have details of where and when the parents were married; however, the birth certificate of another child born in 1855 or after 1860 *will* include this information. Information about marriages given on birth certificates are often detailed and if the parents were married in Ireland or England, you may be told in what parish this event took place. This is of particular value in the case of those who came to Scotland from Ireland or England and may be the only source of information as to their district of origin.

- Ages at marriage may not be stated accurately. If the bride was older than her husband, she may have subtracted a few years.

- Statutory certificates (birth, marriage or death) may indicate that a couple were married – referring to a woman by her married name followed by her maiden name ('M.S.') – but this is sometimes a cover-up of illegitimacy.

- Witnesses at the wedding were often close relatives – a brother or sister. Their names may provide clues to follow back.

Deaths

- Look carefully at the relationship of the informant to the deceased. This may indicate how reliable the details given on the certificate are. A neighbour – or a grandson providing the names of his great-grandparents – may make mistakes.

- Ages are frequently given incorrectly.

- Descriptions of occupation of the deceased person or of his/her parents may not be accurate. The tendency is to put them higher in the social scale than was the truth. A hawker might appear as a merchant, a labourer as a farmer.

- If a person married more than once, the names of all spouses should be entered on the death certificate but are often omitted. If the deceased person is described as 'married to', it usually indicates that the spouse or second spouse is still alive. Occasionally errors are made in this description.

- When looking through the indexes for a death, remember that particularly in modern times – and sometimes earlier – a person may have died in hospital away from home – or may have moved in with a married son or daughter. If therefore you fail to find a death in the district where the family had been living, enlarge your horizons.

A LOST ANCESTOR

If your quarry remains completely lost, consider whether you have omitted to search under all possible spelling variants of the surname or whether the Christian name you have included could be wrong. Recheck the computer index for the missing entry. If you have used the cross-referencing facility for the death of a married woman or for a marriage, search the indexes under the married name of the woman only and for the marriage under the name of the bride and of the bridegroom individually.

There are still a few faults in the computerisation of the indexes. Some entries have been omitted and others typed incorrectly. If you are certain that an ancestor was born, married or died in a particular year in a specific district, check the district book index. Each registration book (of births, deaths, marriages) for each year has an integral index to all entries in the book. This is on a separate fiche – at the end of the section covering the entries in the book. If you do not know the district where the event took place, ask the search room supervisor for access to the 'Paper Index' – the original manuscript or printed index from which the computer indexes were compiled – for births, deaths or marriages of a particular year. You can then check whether an entry has been omitted. If you do find this is so, report it to the supervisor so that the computer index can be corrected.

4 CENSUS RETURNS

Censuses were taken in Scotland every ten years from 1801 onwards but the returns of 1801, 1811, 1821 and 1831 were, in the main, only head counts. Few returns have survived – though session clerks sometimes entered the figures in kirk session minutes. There are some nominal listings for a small number of parishes, usually found with the other records of the kirk session in the National Archives of Scotland (often titled 'List of Inhabitants'). Others are located in local authority archives, or libraries. The amount of information given varies in these early enumerations. Some include ages, place of residence, occupation and names of those within the household. Other returns only refer to the head of each household. A list of parishes which have communion rolls, lists of families and early census returns kept in the National Archives of Scotland with other kirk session material is given in the June 1988 edition of the *Scottish Genealogist*.

In Scotland, the census schedules for 1841, 1851, 1861, 1871, 1881 and 1891 are at present open for consultation. There is (as in England) a 100-year closure on access to the records and thus the 1901 census will be opened in the year 2002. All the census returns have been microfilmed and copies of the returns for the whole of Scotland can be consulted in New Register House. Elsewhere, many archives and libraries have microfilm copies of censuses covering a particular locality or wider area.

A census was taken for each district of Scotland which usually – but not always – corresponded to the parish division. Boundary changes, however, meant that a place included in one census area in one enumeration might be found in a different one in the next. Parishes on the border of two counties or districts which had detached sections in a different county can also pose problems. For example, one part might be in Aberdeenshire and another part in Banffshire, but the whole may be included simply under Aberdeenshire. Details of the boundary changes that came after the work of the Boundary Commission of 1889 are given in *Boundaries of the Counties and Parishes in Scotland 1892*.

Each census for a given area is divided into a number of individual books, covering a section of that district. At the beginning of each book there is a description of the part of the district which is included in it. Sometimes this is very detailed – listing each farm or street – but in others it will only tell you that the area between one street and another or the land between two bounds is included, so do not rely on this as the ultimate guide to what is in the book.

Institutions – prisons, poor houses or hospitals for example – are listed at the end of each enumeration.

CENSUS SEARCHING AIDS

1881 AND 1891 CENSUS INDEXES

The 1881 and 1891 censuses for the whole of Scotland have now been indexed. They are an extremely useful searching tool but, like most indexes, they are not perfect. There are a number of omissions and mis-readings.

The 1881 Census Index

This is available on fiche (at many local archives and libraries) and also on computer in New Register House.

You can search the computer index for a particular name within a selected county or for the whole of Scotland, within age limits if desired. All possible names will be shown on the screen, giving age, parish of birth and reference number of the district, book and page where the entry is recorded. Having found an entry of possible interest, most of the entry for the individual will come up on the screen. Alternatively, the names of all members of that household can be shown.

The Church of Jesus Christ of Latter-Day Saints have issued a set of CDs containing the 1881 British Census and national index, covering England, Scotland, Wales, the Channel Islands, Isle of Man and Royal Navy.

The 1891 Census Index

This can be consulted on computer in New Register House or on the Internet through Scots Origins. The index entries contain the name (surname and forename), sex, age and enumeration district. Digital images of the census, linked to the index, have been available since July 2000 in New Register House and from 2001 the whole census, as well as the index, will be online. The microfilm copy of the census in New Register House will no longer be available.

There is no fiche copy of the 1891 census index.

CONSULT THE ORIGINAL

Always take time to read the full entry of the census as it may contain
valuable extra information which will provide further clues in your
research.

CENSUS INDEXES 1841–71

A great deal of work is being carried out locally in indexing earlier
census returns. A local library, archive or family history society
will be able to give you information on what has been done.
Many local family history centres hold microfilm copies of the
census returns for the district.

For most large towns and cities in Scotland there are *street
indexes* which will give the number of the book within each census
which contains the returns for a certain address. These are indis-
pensable searching aids as returns for the bigger cities may be made
up of a great many books which would take a long time to search.

There is a three-volume 'Index' to the census schedules in
most of the search rooms in New Register House – 1841–51 (the
districts are arranged alphabetically within each county),
1861–71 and 1881–91 (in both these volumes arranged alphabetically by parish for the whole of Scotland). These 'Indexes'
indicate the number of books that cover each district, and
whether there is a street index. The 'Index' gives the reference
number of each census – usually the same as the old parish register number and that given to the post 1854-registration district.

In New Register House, fill in a yellow slip (there is a pad on your desk) with the year and registration number of the census that you want to consult and, in the case of large cities, the book within that return, and then go and collect your reel of microfilm. In country districts, several districts may be included in the same film, while the returns for large cities may take up several reels of film. Make sure you are looking at the right section.

Some of the film of the census returns is, unfortunately, of very bad quality. If you find an entry which is essential to your research and you cannot read it, consult the supervisor in the search room who may be able to consult the original record for you.

INFORMATION GIVEN IN THE CENSUS SCHEDULES

1841 Census (taken 7 June 1841)

Details given in this census are much less informative than in the later ones. The return states:

- The names of the occupants of the household (no relationships within the household are given)

- Their ages – but in most cases the ages of adults are only given to within five years, rounded down: thus 40 = 40–44

- The occupations of adults within certain broad classes – agricultural labourer, female servant, farmer etc.

- Whether the person was born or not born (indicated by 'Y' (yes) or 'N' (no)) in the county in which he or she was living at the time of taking the census. If born in Ireland, the enumerator marked the paper with 'I', or in England with 'E'

- Households are divided by //. If unrelated persons were living with the family, they are divided off by a single /.

1851 Census (taken 31 March 1851)

The amount of information given in the censuses from 1851 onwards improves enormously. For each household, the return states:

- The names of the occupants, giving the relationship of each person to the head of the household
- Age of each member of the household
- The status of each person – widow, widower, unmarried, married
- The occupation of each person
- The parish of birth of each member of the household
- Whether the occupant was blind, deaf or dumb.

Later Censuses

The 1861 Census (taken 8 April 1861) was similar to the 1851 census but with the additional information:

- The number of children in the household at school
- The number of rooms with one or more windows inhabited by the family.

The 1871 Census (taken 3 April 1871) and the 1881 Census (taken 4 April 1881) were similar to the previous census. The 1891 Census (taken 6 April 1891) was similar to the previous census but with the additional information of whether individuals spoke only Gaelic or both Gaelic and English.

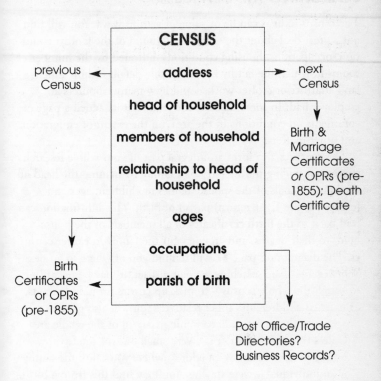

CENSUS

previous ← Census

address

→ next Census

head of household

members of household

Birth & Marriage Certificates *or* OPRs (pre-1855); Death Certificate

relationship to head of household

ages

occupations

Birth Certificates or OPRs (pre-1855) ←

parish of birth

Post Office/Trade Directories? Business Records?

Census – Where Next?

SEARCHING THE CENSUSES

The census returns can be of value in various ways. You will find out a great deal about the social background of the family: education, occupations, housing conditions indicated by the number of rooms in which the family lived, possibly details of how much land a farmer or crofter worked and how many labourers an employer had. In some districts the enumerators added a page of comments on conditions in the area, on the extent of emigration and other matters.

The censuses also form an integral part of your whole research strategy in tracing the ancestry of a family by naming the head of the house, details of the spouse, names of children, ages and (except for the 1841 return) parish of birth. This information can lead back to the birth certificates of all members of the household, to their deaths, and an entry for the family in earlier censuses. The diagram on page 57 will remind you of where to go next. Whenever you are searching a small district, it may be rewarding to search the whole census – to pick up entries for grandparents, or married children and other relatives. You will also gain an insight into the social and economic make-up of the whole area.

Unless the census district is a very small one, or indexed by person, you need to know an address where you think the family – or an individual – were staying. You may find this from a birth, marriage or death certificate, from a legal document, town directory, communion roll or monumental inscription.

Post Office or other directories (which for many towns date back to the 1840s and earlier) may list shopkeepers, or those of some means. Entries in these directories depended on payment

MAKE THE MOST OF THE 1881 AND 1891 CENSUS INDEXES

If you are not sure whether someone was dead or alive by 1881 or 1891, search the index for that year to check the possibilities.

An entry identified in one of the indexed censuses may also help you to find the family in an earlier return.

being made – so do not expect miners or labourers to be listed. Get in touch with the local public library of the district in which you are interested as they will probably have local directories on their shelves. There are good runs of the Edinburgh Post Office Directories and microfiche copies of the Glasgow Post Office Directories in New Register House – as well as some for Aberdeen and Dundee. Consult *Scottish Trades and Professions* compiled by D.R. Torrance, which has a section on Scottish directories.

Information given in one census may guide you to one ten years earlier. If in 1881 the family were staying in Campbeltown but you see that there was a nine-year-old and also an eleven-year-old in the household born in Southend, then the birth certificates of these children will give you addresses where the family were living. You then know where to look for them in the 1871 census.

TROUBLE-SHOOTING IN THE CENSUSES

As in all other aspects of family history research, the census returns can present a challenge in determining whether the listed family is the one you were looking for and it is important to establish this. *It is essential to make sure that you are following the right family.*

The following are some of the problems which may arise:

- If you find a family which looks right but the mother's name is wrong or there are children too old to have been born to a known marriage, consider the possibility that the head of the household had married twice. Look then for evidence of this other marriage in the statutory registers or Old Parish Registers.

- Take time to locate the family in as many census returns as possible. Information taken down by the enumerators was not always correct and you may find conflicting evidence of age or parish of birth in different returns. If possible, compare the names and ages of members of the household in several returns to make sure that there is some correlation. It is important to gather as much information as you can to assess the scope of your future investigations.

- Married women or widows are sometimes listed under their maiden names.

- In some areas – such as the fishing villages of the north-east – one or two surnames predominate which can make it difficult to select the right entry. Heads of households may be distinguished in some communities by the addition of a nickname.

- Many families moved house frequently and particularly in large cities this can make it difficult to find them. You may find an address from a child's birth certificate, registered in January of the year when a census was taken, only to find that the family had moved before the enumerator came round a few months later. Often, however, they did not move far and it is always worth going through the rest of the book which contained the address you were checking and perhaps the other books covering the immediate area. In some returns, parts of the same street may be listed in widely separated enumeration books and you will need to check these. The street indexes will indicate if this is so, and give the relevant book numbers.

- If you know the occupation of the head of the house – perhaps as a miner or as a worker in a chemical works – you may be able to locate his place of work and can then search the streets in the vicinity as he would almost certainly have lived within walking distance of his employment.

- Occasionally you will find that a town address given for a family – such as a vennel or wynd – is not listed in the street index for that district for that return. You will then have to do some research on a town map or in another street index to try to identify where the place is. Post Office Directories may help as these have a section indexed by street, marking where vennels or lanes lead off the main thoroughfare.

- Check that the farm or township where you think a family or individual lived is listed in the census you are searching. If on the border of a parish or county, it may be included in a different enumeration.

- A few of the 1841 census returns have been lost. There are no extant enumerations for the Fife parishes of Abdie, Auchtermuchty, Balmerino, Ceres, Collessie, Creich, Cults, Cupar, Dairsie, Dunbog, Kinghorn, Kinglassie, Kirkcaldy, Leslie and Auchinleck, Ayrshire. The 1881 return for Dunscore is missing, as is the second half of the 1881 census for Dumfries.

- If you lose a member of the family – perhaps a widower –
  think laterally. Where might he have gone? Perhaps he went to
  stay with a married son or daughter. If you can locate that
  household, you may find him.

VALUATION ROLLS

From 1855 till 1974, valuation rolls were compiled annually for
all heritable property in every part of Scotland, county by county,
with the burghs being listed separately. A description is given of
each piece of property with details of the proprietor, the tenant,
occupier, inhabitant occupier and the valuation. However, occupiers of lands rented at less than £4 per year were not listed.
Valuation Rolls are kept in the National Archives of Scotland (the
class reference number is 'VR') but copies of the valuations of a
particular district will also be found in local archives and libraries.

The importance of these valuation rolls to the family historian
is that you may be able to see year by year how long a family
remained at a given address (if they were in the 'listed' category)
and also to confirm at a glance whether they were proprietors,
tenants or occupiers.

The rolls, however, include no information which will lead you
to finding out where the family lived before or where they moved
to. Another difficulty is that, lacking indexes to persons, it may be
hard to track down a particular family. There are only a few
indexes to streets – the repertory in the National Archives of
Scotland marks the districts which are indexed – and without a
searching aid, it may not be worth spending the time looking for
a particular family.

5 THE OLD PARISH REGISTERS

Before 1855 the main genealogical source of family history in Scotland is the parish registers of the Church of Scotland. All the surviving registers of 901 parishes, amounting to about 3500 registers, are in the keeping of the Registrar General for Scotland but microfilm copies have been made which are accessible to the public in New Register House. Many libraries and family history centres throughout the world have also acquired microfilm copies of the Old Parish Registers.

Some of the registers are badly written and it is important to take great care when you are reading them. In a number of areas, the microfilm of the register is poor in quality and is very difficult to read. In the cause of protecting the originals, it is no longer possible to consult the originals but if you have problems, consult a member of staff in the search room in New Register House who may be able to check a particular entry in the original register.

THE OPRS – A USEFUL SOURCE

These records of birth and baptism, proclamation and marriage, death and some burials were kept by the session clerk of each parish (often the schoolmaster) or the minister. In most cases, one register will contain records of births and baptisms for a particular period at the front, followed by marriages and then deaths and burials – if any records are extant. In some parishes, however, there are separate registers for baptisms and for marriages and in others, records of all the events may be intermingled.

There is a *List of the Parish Registers* in the search rooms in New Register House which will show you what each volume of the parish registers contains and what years are covered, as well as giving the number of the parish and the number of each volume. If you are searching in New Register House, you will need to check this catalogue when filling out your slip prior to collecting your reel of microfilm – you may take out two reels at a time. Put down the number of the parish, followed by the number of the volume you wish to search.

These registers formed an integral part of the records kept by the parish, such as kirk session minutes or accounts and in some parishes you may find fragments of records of baptisms, marriages and burials with the minutes or accounts, rather than entered in the registers of these events. Some of these additional records have been filmed and are in New Register House as part of the OPRs

---

CHARACTER OF THE OPRS

The form and content of the parish registers is very different from that of the statutory registers and demands some new research techniques. Remember that:

- Registration was not compulsory.

- Dates of commencement of the registers vary widely and a great many of the registers are deficient – either having been badly kept at certain periods or not having been kept at all.

- They were mainly concerned with Church of Scotland members.

- There was no standard form of entry.

---

but others are in the National Archives of Scotland with the collection of kirk session records for that parish. There is a list of these additional parish records at the back of the *List of the Old Parish Registers* in New Register House and a note of the addenda is given against the *List* entry for the particular parish.

In the case of large parishes, the microfilm of the registers covers several reels, and on the other hand, one reel may contain the complete registers of several small parishes. Always make sure that you are reading the right section of the film, covering the parish in which you are interested.

Non-compulsory registration

The first great difference between the statutory registers and the OPRs is that before 1855 there was no legal obligation to record births or baptisms, proclamations or marriages or deaths and burials – and a great many such events went unrecorded. As the influence of the Church of Scotland in local communities declined in the 18th and 19th centuries – due to the number of break-away churches, increased secularisation of society and greater mobility of the population – the number of entries made decreased. In 1783 a Stamp Act was passed putting a tax of 3d on every entry made in the parish registers. This acted as a direct disincentive to registration and the Act was not repealed till 1794. A statement made in connection with the population abstract of 1801 revealed that out of 850 parishes which made returns to the Government, only 99 possessed registers which were regularly kept, the rest having only occasional entries or no register at all. In the light of all this, it is surprising how much can be found in the parish registers.

Surviving OPRs

The earliest date of extant registers for each parish varies widely. The oldest parish register is that for the Perthshire parish of Errol which starts in 1553. Only 21 parishes have registers which date before 1600. A further 127 registers date to between 1600 and 1650, with 266 beginning between 1650 and 1700 and another 226 going back to the period between 1700 and 1750. None of the registers of Skye or the Outer Isles commenced before 1800.

A number of registers have been lost or destroyed over the centuries – through fire, flood, damp, the ravages of mice or human action. The older registers for Halkirk in Caithness are said 'to have been destroyed many years ago by some ill-disposed persons', while an early register of births and marriages for the Fife parish of Inverkeithing was discovered recently among Court of Session papers having been used as evidence in a court case.

Another problem of the OPRs is that many of the records were very badly kept at one time or another. Session clerks sometimes retaliated for non-payment of their fees by taking away the register for a period of time or failing to make entries in it. Some record-keepers were inefficient, with wrong names, places or dates copied into the book, and many registers are blank over certain periods of years. Entries might also be put in the wrong place or the baptisms of several children recorded together in a composite entry. Particularly in the two or three decades before 1855, many parents who had previously failed to record the births or baptisms of their children knowing that statutory registration was to be introduced in January 1855, made up for their omissions in 1854. In many parish registers there are many pages of 'late entries' in this year.

RECORDS OF THE CHURCH OF SCOTLAND

In the main, the Old Parish Registers were the records of the Church of Scotland – the reformed church which was established in Scotland at the Reformation in 1560 when the national church ceased to be Roman Catholic. A long struggle for supremacy between the presbyterian and episcopalian factions in the Church was ultimately resolved in the Act of Union of 1707, which saw the presbyterians emerge victorious. From the genealogical point of view, however, the point to remember is that whether the Church had an episcopal or presbyterian bias, the records of the parishes over this period were the Old Parish Registers.

A number of persons who belonged to dissenting congregations – as well as Episcopalians – did record baptisms and proclamation or marriage in the OPRs, sometimes duplicating the entry in the register of their own congregation. A few Roman Catholic proclamations can also be found in the parish registers.

CONTENT OF THE REGISTERS

Unlike the statutory registers where the form and content of the certificates were laid down, what was recorded in each parish register was left to the session clerk or minister who kept it. The standard of recording and the amount of information given in each entry varies widely from parish to parish, and from time to time.

Births & Baptisms

The more important church event was baptism rather than birth. In some registers the dates of both events are given. Where there is a date without an indication whether this record concerned a birth or baptism, assume that it referred to the baptism. Baptism sometimes took place on the day of birth and usually within a few days or weeks – though occasionally it might be delayed for some considerable time.

Information which you may find given in a baptismal certificate *may* include:

- The name of the child
- The name of the child's father and usually – but not always – the name of the child's mother, giving her maiden name
- Occupation of the father
- Where the family were living
- Date of baptism and/or birth
- Witnesses to the baptism.

In some entries only the name of the child, the date of baptism and the name of the father are given. If there are two fathers sharing the same Christian name and surname, it may be hard to sort out the families. Details of residence may be the deciding factor.

Proclamations & Marriages

The proclamation was often recorded rather than the date of the actual marriage – but in some entries both are noted. The proclamation of the forthcoming marriage was supposed to be declared three times in the parish church – usually on succeeding Sabbaths – but this obligation was often waived on payment of a fee and the three proclamations were made at the same time.

Many marriages were what was termed 'irregular' or 'clandestine' – performed in front of witnesses, without due proclamation of banns or by someone other than the local minister. Such marriages – which were very common – were quite legal though frowned upon by the Church of Scotland. Sometimes an entry in the parish register indicates that an irregular marriage had taken place but more often an entry will be found in the kirk session records of the parish, recorded either as an appearance by the guilty parties before the session or as a payment of a fine for their misdeeds. In the case of a 'missing' marriage, it is always worth looking in the kirk session minutes or accounts for the relevant parish around the time the first known child was baptised.

In the case of a 'regular' proclamation and marriage, information which *may* be present in the OPR entry includes:

- Dates of proclamations (which sometimes were recorded on two or three Sabbaths but more usually were noted in one entry)
- Date of marriage and sometimes the name of the minister
- The names of the man and the woman
- The parish of each and sometimes the place of residence
- The occupation of the man
- Very occasionally the name of the bride's father and rarely also the name of the bridegroom's father
- Occasionally the names of the cautioners (often relatives) for each party, who gave up pledges at the time of the proclamation for the good behaviour of both man and woman. These pledges could be redeemed when the marriage was duly performed
- The names of witnesses.

TWO PROCLAMATION ENTRIES

If the marriage or proclamations of a couple are recorded in two parishes, always consult both entries. One session clerk may be more generous than the other in the amount of information he includes in his register.

If the man and the woman lived in different parishes, the proclamation may be recorded twice – in the parish of residence of both man and woman. The dates may not be the same – one may refer to a proclamation and another to the actual marriage – or the proclamation may have been given out on different days in the two parishes.

Deaths & Burials

Death and burial registers were the least well-kept of the parish records and for many parishes there are none before the statutory registers. As with the other registers, the information given in an OPR entry – which more often concerns the burial rather than the death – varies greatly. It is often disappointing in recording only the date of burial and the cost of the hire of the mortcloth – the pall owned by the parish and hired out at the funeral to cover the coffin. Many people did not have the means to pay for a mortcloth and many children's burials went unrecorded for this reason.

In some entries, age at death, cause of death, residence and occupation are given and occasionally very full details are included about the circumstances of the death.

INDEXES TO THE OPRS

All births and baptisms, proclamations and marriages recorded in the Old Parish Registers have now been indexed – but not the deaths and burials. Work is in hand to index all the burial records in the OPRs and there is a list in New Register House of the parish registers for which indexes to burials have been completed:

- The indexes to births/baptisms show the name of the child, the names of both parents (if given in the register), the date of baptism (marked C) or birth (marked B) and the parish in which the entry is recorded, with its reference number and volume number.

- The indexes to marriages show the names of both parties, the date of marriage (or proclamation) and the parish register in which the event is recorded, with its reference number and volume number.

After many of the index entries, you will see a reference 'FR' plus a number which refers to a frame number on the microfilm copy of the register. This may be a very useful in locating an entry, particularly in the case of those recorded out of chronological order (such as late entries). Always take note of the frame number. Unfortunately, in a great many cases, this frame number (on the top of each frame) was not highlighted when the register was filmed and it is unreadable.

If you are searching the registers of a large city, such as Glasgow or Edinburgh, it is always wise to check the GRO *List of the Old Parish Registers* (which is available in the search rooms of New Register House) to confirm that the computer's reference to the volume number is correct. There are a number of errors especially in the case of registers for the cities. The GRO *List* is arranged by county (starting at the north of Scotland and working down) and details the dates and events (births, marriages, deaths) covered by each register for each parish.

Computer or Fiche Indexes

The OPR indexes are available in several forms, described here.

COMPUTER INDEXES

OPR indexes are stored on computer in New Register House and are also available through any centre which has a computer link-up with New Register House and through the GRO website. These indexes can be searched year by year, covering the whole of Scotland, for a birth/baptism or proclamation/marriage *or* in ten-year periods (1800–09, 1810–19, for example) for either category within a certain county. Several of the small counties adjacent to each other are grouped together. The entry on the screen will give you the reference number for the parish register and the number of the volume in which the entry occurs. Names are indexed according to their spelling and Mc and Mac are indexed separately. There is a 'like-sounding' facility on the computer which will bring up many alternative spellings of surnames – but not all.

The computer index arranged by county and decade is particularly useful if you want to collect all children born to a particular couple over a decade: key in a surname (without an initial or Christian name), and search for males and females. These are separated on the index though the computer often fails to distinguish the sex of the child and boys and girls may be intermingled. Even when this appears to be the case, the indexes to both males *and* females should be searched. All entries of baptism under that surname within the parishes in that county – or group of counties – over a period of ten years will come up on your screen, making it possible to find the relevant ones as the parents' names are given. It is also a useful guide to the number of families of a particular surname recording their children at the time in the area. Remember that the lack of a mother's name may make it appear that one father had a very large family.

FICHE INDEXES

OPR indexes are also available on fiche arranged by county (there are separate fiches for baptisms and marriages. This is the most reliable of the indexes (though there are some omissions and errors). Every name is indexed as it appears in the register. This is helpful in that you can see the various spelling variants. On the fiche index Mc and Mac are indexed under one heading. On the other hand, it may take much longer to work through this index if you are collecting all the children (Christian names unknown) born to a particular family. The fiche reference will indicate whether the date given is for a birth (B) or baptism (C). Some frame numbers are given – particularly in cases where the event has been recorded out of chronological order.

THE INTERNATIONAL GENEALOGICAL INDEX

The International Genealogical Index (IGI) includes most (but not all) entries taken from the index to the parish registers – and it may also include some entries taken from registers of dissenting congregations or extracted from submissions by members of the LDS church. Spelling of surnames is given in the index as it appears in the original but the entries are grouped according to a stardardised form of the surname. This can be very helpful when looking for a name which has many variant spellings. There have been several editions of the IGI and there are some differences between them – with entries added or erased. If you cannot find an entry for which you are looking, check the OPR fiche indexes.

CD-ROM

Scottish Church Records are available on CD-ROM through the LDS family history centres and in New Register House. This can be a quick way to collect all children born to a named couple anywhere in Scotland – but remember that there may be more than one couple who have the same surnames and Christian names.

Consider which index will serve your purposes best. If the surname you are researching is one which has few spelling variants, then the computer index will probably be the quickest and easiest to use. However, if you are faced with a name which has many alternative spellings, consult the fiche index – and always use this to back up and check your findings on the computer index or on the LDS indexes.

RESEARCH WARNING

Never jump to conclusions that an index entry is relevant. Always consult the full text in the register.

RESEARCH STRATEGIES – WORKING WITH THE OPRS

For most people, the way into the parish registers will be through the statutory registers – from a marriage or death certificate recorded after 1854 – with perhaps additional information gained from a census entry:

- A census entry will give the age of the person concerned and parish of birth.
- The post-1854 death or marriage certificate will name the parents of the ancestor and confirm the approximate date of birth given on the census.

Armed with these details you can consult the indexes to the parish registers and find the right entry for the birth and then go on to locate the marriage of the child's parents. Take time to find as many siblings as possible. Given the uneven quality of entries in the parish registers, one baptismal entry may only name the child's father, but the baptism of a later child (written perhaps by a different session clerk) may show the name of the child's mother, where the family were living and include the names of witnesses.

It is customary to find no more than about 18 months or two years between the birth of each child and if there is a gap of four or more years (unless it is at the end of a time of child-bearing), it is worth going back to see whether you have missed one – though the mother may have had a child who died soon after birth or who was still-born and not registered. It is not unusual however, particularly if the family moved from parish to parish, to find some children's births and baptisms recorded and others omitted.

TWO CHILDREN OF THE SAME NAME

If a child died in infancy it was the custom for a later child to be given the same Christian name. In Highland areas, however, it was not uncommon for several brothers or sisters – all surviving – to be given the same Christian name. They were usually differentiated by nicknames.

Practising Research Techniques

Take the case of a James Morrison who died in Newton, Ayr in 1878 at the age of 84, son of John Morrison and Flora Cuthbert, and known to have been born in Ayr. A search of the parish register index shows that his birth and baptism were duly recorded in the parish register in 1794 and the marriage of his parents took place there in 1793. You can assume that John was aged at least 17 when he married and therefore he would have been born before 1776. It is unlikely (though not impossible) that he was still alive after 1854 and therefore there will be no death certificate for him.

The next step would be to see if there were burial records for the parish where he was last living and to look for monumental inscriptions, to try to establish an approximate year of birth.

Unless John could be found in a census (giving an indication of his age), you may then be faced with the problem of searching prior to 1776 for his birth without knowing where this took place or when and with no indication as to the names of his parents. There may be no entry of possible relevance anywhere nearby or you may discover that there were several John Morrisons born in the right district over a possible period of years. You then have to try to prove whether one of these entries is the relevant one.

FACING THE PROBLEMS

If you find no entry of possible relevance for the birth or marriage of an ancestor in the OPRs, you can take the following steps to try to determine why you came up against a blank wall:

- Look at the *Detailed list of the Old Parochial Registers of Scotland*, first published in 1872 and reprinted as *Key to the Parochial Registers of Scotland* by Ben Bloxham. Copies of the *Detailed List* are in the Search Rooms of New Register House. This book lists the registers of each parish (including burials) and indicates the main blanks and other deficiencies in each volume. It does not cover every gap or imperfection but it is a very useful guide to the condition of the registers. A note that the registers for the parish where your ancestor is known to have been born have no extant marriage records for some years prior to his birth may account for the fact that you cannot find his parents' marriage or proclamation. Similarly, failure to find a birth in an area where later generations of a family were settled may be explained by a missing or defective register rather than by the fact that the family had moved into the district from elsewhere.

- Look carefully at the register of the parish where the family was last sighted. Was it carefully kept? Does it appear that there were not many entries and that the session clerk might have failed in his duties?

- Were there other families of the same surname recording the baptisms of their children and marriages in the parish where the last known ancestor lived? If the latter appears to be the only head of family of that name, it is very possible that he moved into the area from elsewhere.

- Were there any reasons why the family might have moved – such as clearance from Highland areas in the late 18th and early 19th centuries or movement from the Highlands to the central districts of Scotland in search of work?

- Look at a map and see whether the family lived in a parish on the borders of one county and another and make sure that you extend your search to cover the parishes of both counties.

- Might the family have belonged to a dissenting congregation? If you find that the family (on the evidence of statutory marriage certificates) belonged to the Free Church, the United Presbyterian Church or were Roman Catholics, then this may be the reason why a marriage or baptisms of children were not entered in the OPRs.

FOLLOWING UP THE CLUES

On the positive side, there are clues in the parish registers which can be followed up to try to determine which one of several possible entries is the right one:

- Some families – particularly farming folk – often remained in the same area for generations. If you find an entry of possible relevance for a child born in a township where later generations lived, there is a strong possibility that this is the right line.

- The names of witnesses to baptisms often provide valuable clues as they may be relatives – either the grandparents or uncles and aunts of the child. When looking for the birth of that child's father, look to see if the latter had a father or siblings whose names appear as witnesses in the later generation. In the same way, the cautioner sometimes mentioned at a proclamation, was often a relative of bride or groom.

- The person you are tracing may have acted as witness to the baptisms of children in another family of the same surname. This may indicate the two families were related and may be an important clue when researching the preceding generation.

- Take into account the traditional Scottish naming patterns. Not all families followed this pattern but many did:
  ❏ The first son was named after his paternal grandfather.
  ❏ The second son was named after his maternal grandfather.
  ❏ The third son was named after his father.
  ❏ The first daughter was named after her maternal grandmother.
  ❏ The second daughter was named after her paternal grandmother.
  ❏ The third daughter was named after her mother.

- Note any unusual Christian names which are handed down from generation to generation.

- If a child has a middle name, it may be the maiden name of the mother, grandmother or other relative. The child may, however, be called after the local landowner or the minister of the parish.

RECORDS OF UNITED PRESBYTERIAN & FREE CHURCH CONGREGATIONS

If you cannot find an entry in the parish registers, consider whether the family might have belonged to a dissenting congregation.

During the 18th and 19th centuries, the Church of Scotland suffered many divisions due to disputes over patronage – the rights of lay patrons to appoint ministers – and over various theological arguments. The diagram of the various splits in the church on page 287 shows the main divisions. The most important ones to note when carrying out genealogical research are:

- The Episcopal Church which became a separate entity in 1690

- The First Secession of 1733 (which in turn split into Burghers and Anti-burghers, New Lichts and Auld Lichts), known as the Associate Synod after 1747

- The Relief Church of 1761

- The Free Church of 1843

- The United Presbyterian Church – formed by a union of many of the secession churches in the second half of the 19th century, in 1900 joined by the Free Church.

If you do not know to which church the family belonged, take time to research the religious 'make-up' of the parish where they lived. Consult the *First (or Old) Statistical Account* – compiled in the 1790s and the *Second (or New) Statistical Account* – compiled in the 1840s. These Accounts were contributed by the minister of each parish and dealt with many aspects of life in the parish, including comments on population, farming, names of heritors, life of the people and ecclesiastical make-up of the parish. The reports vary in the amount of information given but are often useful in showing the proportion of members of the Church of Scotland to members of dissenting congregations.

The *Ordnance Gazetteer of Scotland* edited by Francis H. Groome lists the churches in each parish, and when they were built. This gazetteer and the *Statistical Accounts* will be found in most larger Scottish libraries or archives.

The largest collection of records of the dissenting Churches is in the National Archives of Scotland and this is where you should go first. If there are no records for the churches in which you are interested there, they may be in the local authority archives or still with the particular congregation.

Many of these churches have no extant baptismal, marriage or burial records – though there may be session minutes or lists of communicants and church members.

In the National Archives of Scotland, first consult the catalogue for *Records of the Church of Scotland and other Presbyterian Churches* (CH) in the Index Room. It is divided into several sections:

- Records of the General Assembly (CH1)
- Other records of the Church of Scotland (CH2) – Synods and Presbyteries
- Records of the kirk sessions of the Church of Scotland (CH2)
- Records of the United Presbyterian Church (CH3) – which include records of all the congregations which came together before 1900 – Associate Synod, Relief Church, Burgher and Anti-burghers.
- Records of the Free Church (CH3)
- Records of the United Original Secession (CH3)
- Records of the Reformed Presbyterian Church (CH3).

For records of dissenting congregations, check the last four sections of the catalogue listed under the alphabetical list of parishes given in each section. This will name all the congregations for which the NAS holds records and give you the class reference – CH3 plus a number. Then go to the CH3 repertories on the shelf (arranged in numerical order) and look up the entry under the number given in the catalogue. This will give detailed information about the contents of the holding – whether there are registers of baptisms or marriages and if so, what years are covered and what other records make up the holding. Fill in a slip and order up the volume you want – CH3 + the number of the holding + the number of the particular volume within the collection.

If there are no records listed for a particular church, get in touch with the relevant local authority archive (check the parish list on page 218 to find under which local authority it comes.)

Some records previously held by the NAS have been re-transmitted to the local authority archives but microfilm copies have been retained in Edinburgh. This is marked on the detailed repertory with 'M'. The microfilms can be read in the National Archives of Scotland.

RECORDS OF OTHER CHURCHES

There are individual repertories in the National Archives of Scotland for the records of churches of some other denominations held there. Look at the first page of each repertory to see what parishes are included.

- **Roman Catholic Church** (RH21) The NAS holds photocopies of a number of registers of baptisms, marriages and deaths –

arranged by diocese. There is an alphabetical list of parishes at
the beginning of the repertory. Most Roman Catholic registers
do not start until the 19th century. Photocopies of the originals
are usually also to be found in the parish concerned, while the
Archdiocese of Glasgow holds most of the originals. A booklet
entitled *Catholic Missions and Registers 1700–1880* (Volume 6 –
Scotland) compiled by Michael Gandy provides a guide to
what records are extant and where to find them. There are very
few Roman Catholic records for the 18th century but there are
interesting lists of those then termed 'Papists' (i.e. Roman
Catholics) in the records of the General Assembly (in the NAS,
class reference CH1) taken in many parts of Scotland circa
1708-28. In many cases these list everyone in the household
and sometimes name a Protestant relative who was held
'responsible' for the Catholic members of the family.

- **Quakers** (CH10) There is a typed list of births, marriages and
deaths 1622–1890, compiled by S. Strath Maxwell.

- **Methodists** (CH11)

- **Episcopal Church** (CH12) The catalogue lists the records
held in the NAS. The records of many Episcopal churches are
still held in the parishes or in other archives. Also search the
National Register of Archives list of surveys (see page 87) to
check whether there are records for the parish you want which
have been surveyed. These records will not be in the NAS.

- **United Free Church** (CH13)

- **Congregational Church** (CH14)

- **Unitarian Church** (CH15)

6 Route Finding –
Beyond The OPRs

For many people, family history research stops at the parish registers but there is an enormous amount of material beyond the parish registers of great value to the family historian in two ways:

- In providing information which will lead back into the parish registers, prove the relevance of an entry found there or extend genealogical knowledge of earlier generations
- In filling out the family history and putting flesh on the bones of people of the past.

Having exhausted the possibilities of the parish registers and being faced with either no ancestral line or several which might – or might not – be relevant, it is time to take stock of what other sources are available to break the impasse or provide more information on the family.

The choice of source material is bewildering and it is important to work out a strategy of research by assessing what is known about your ancestor or family in asking the following questions:

- What did he or she do?
- Where did he or she live?
- When did he or she live?

Records are made by the contact of an individual with a group of people or organisation – social, legal or economic – and so you need to take account of the milieu in which your ancestor moved.

Knowledge of the class of society in which he or she lived will be a deciding factor in the selection of records, as well as in a consideration of the most immediate authority in the life of the individual – whether it be the kirk session, the employer, the court which recorded testaments or granted licences or the burgh council.

It is also important to try to evaluate the records before plunging headlong into a search:

- Are there indexes?
- If there are no indexes, how big a task will it be to search the series over a given number of years? Minute books or side heads on the register can be a great help.
- Are there any printed transcriptions or abridgments?
- Are the records written in English, Old Scots or Latin? Some legal documents, particularly the sasine registers, were written in Latin till the 18th century.
- Are the records readable? After about 1700, handwriting changed and many find earlier writing very difficult to read.
- How much information will be found in a particular record?
- What sort of information will be found in a particular record?

Some source material may only provide 'sightings' of your quarry – the occurrence of a name at a time and place which might be relevant. Other documents may provide a 'scent' – a reference which in a context (name of a spouse, age, occupation, relation or residence) is sufficient to determine the relevance of the material and advance the search by providing clues or information. Even 'sightings' may be valuable in building up a body of information which will lead on to the next step in the ancestral hunt.

FIRST CHOICE

Search first those records which you think will provide the richest pickings for the least expenditure of time. What you search later may depend on your expertise and the extent of your dedication to family history research.

WHERE TO FIND THE RECORDS

The first decision is whether to make Edinburgh your first port of call and to go to the National Archives of Scotland or whether it will be more helpful to visit a local archive or library. Work is in progress (2001) under the Scottish Archive Network (SCAN) to create an electronic search room on the internet. This will provide access to catalogues of archival holdings throughout Scotland and beyond, and make it easier to find out what source material is available and where. The website is http://www.scan.org.uk.Many libraries and family history centres also have their own websites which may be very informative.

The National Archives of Scotland (until 1999 known as the Scottish Record Office) are in General Register House (GRH) and should not be confused with the General Register Office (GRO) also known as New Register House which keeps the statutory registers, census returns and parish registers. The National Archives of Scotland have vast holdings of public and private records. At the NAS are the records of central government and proceedings of the highest civil and criminal courts, public records of land ownership (registers of sasines), registers of deeds, records of Sheriff Courts and local courts, church records, private archives, records concerning trade and taxation, valuation rolls, maps and plans.

Local authority archives hold a wide and varied range of records, concerning local administration at all periods, including the records of the burghs, education records, Poor Law records, church records, family and business papers, newspapers, maps and plans. There is an overlap with the National Archives of Scotland holdings as certain classes of records of local interest – such as burgh records and church records – may be in the local authority archives, having been transferred there from the NAS.

Libraries and other archives throughout Scotland also hold both printed material and manuscript material – some of localised or specialised interest.

The National Register of Archives (Scotland) known as the NRA(S), consists of a large series of surveys of records in private hands concerning people, families, businesses and organisations. The catalogues of these collections can be consulted in the National Archives of Scotland, and there is a master index online at http//www.hmc.gov.uk/nra/nra2.htm. Access to any of these documents must be requested through the NAS.

The Scottish Records Association (c/o Dundee City Archives, 21 City Square, Dundee DD1 3BY) publishes a series of *Summaries of Archival Holdings* at most of the main archives and libraries in Scotland. These are very useful as a guide to what is held in each repository. *Exploring Scottish History* edited by Michael Cox also contains a great deal of useful information about what is available and where.

On page 183 there is a list of the main classes of records which you may wish to consult, in the course of research, indicating what sort of material each contains and whether you will find it in national or local archives

RESEARCH IN NAS

The National Archives of Scotland are situated at the east end of Princes Street, Edinburgh – behind the Wellington statue. Wheel-chair access is available. Some classes of records (such as maps and plans, court records and railway records) are kept at West Register House, in Charlotte Square where there is also a Search Room. It is wise to check in advance where the records in which you are in-terested are kept. Due to lack of storage space, many records are now out-housed and have to be ordered up 48 hours in advance so they can be brought to one of the search rooms for you to study.

The NAS and its Search Room at West Register House are both open 9.00 to 16.45 Monday to Friday (except on some public and local holidays). The NAS are usually shut for the first fortnight in November for stocktaking; West Register House is closed for the third week in November. Seats cannot be booked but if you arrive reasonably early, there should be no problems in finding a place.

YOUR FIRST VISIT

The member of staff at the reception desk may ask you what research you want to undertake. Make sure that you can answer this question– it will be sufficient to indicate that you are inter-ested in church records, legal or court records, for example. Many people come to the NAS when they really want to consult the records of New Register House. Due to security regulations, coats, heavy jackets, brief-cases and handbags have to be left at the cloakroom on the ground floor. At West Register House there are lockers in the hall where such items are deposited. Do not bring heavy luggage as there are no storage facilities for such items. Laptop computers are allowed.

On reaching the Historical Reading Room in the National Archives of Scotland or the Search Room at West Register House, a staff member will ask you to fill out a simple form, giving name and address and indicating your research interests. You will need to provide some form of identification (such as driving licence or passport) and you will then be issued with a Reader's Ticket, valid for three years for both Search Rooms. There is no fee. Bring the ticket with you every time you visit the NAS or West Register House, deposit it on the supervisor's desk in the Search Room when you arrive and collect it whenever you leave the building.

You can order up to three items at a time by filling out a slip with the proper reference number on it, your name, seat number and date. The items will usually be brought to you within about 20 minutes. All notes must be taken in pencil – or a laptop computer can be used. Power points are available.

The member of staff who issues your ticket will explain the cataloguing system to you and will always be willing to give you some help on subsequent visits – but it is up to you to find your own way round the archive and do your own research. On your first visit you may find this daunting – but persevere.

Finding Records in the NAS

The records are all given class reference codes – for example, SC covers all the Sheriff Court records, CH includes the church records of most denominations, B is for the burgh records and GD is the section covering Gifts and Deposits. You will find a list of the main classes of records in the National Archives of Scotland which you are likely to use on page 187. Each class of records has its own catalogue or repertory which varies in the amount of descriptive detail given. These class catalogues are arranged alphabetically, according to the class reference letter, round the walls of the NAS Index Room.

First consult the one-volume *Summary Catalogue Index*. This lists alphabetically most of the records held in the NAS and gives the class reference. The *Catalogue* does not, however, include references to the individual church records and for those you have to go straight to the *Records of the Church of Scotland* catalogue. If, for example, you want to consult the Hearth Tax records, check the *Summary Catalogue* under Hearth Tax and you will be told to go to E (for Exchequer records) 69. The repertory for E69 will show you what parishes are covered and the number given to that particular section. Another example: to check whether there are any family papers for Scrymgeour of Glassary, check the *Summary Catalogue* under Scrymgeour and you will find the reference GD (Gifts & Deposits) 137. The individual repertory for GD137 will detail the contents of the collection.

There is also a three-volume *Summary Catalogue* (with red labels on the spine, next to the one-volume *Summary Catalogue Index*) which may sometimes be useful. It gives details of all the records by class. For example – if you look up B – Burgh – it will list all royal burghs for which there are records in the National Archives of Scotland, giving you the number assigned to each burgh. If you look up E – Exchequer – the catalogue will list all the sections of exchequer records such as Farm Horse Tax, Poll Tax or Forfeited Estate Papers and give you the E number which enables you to go to the detailed repertory of those records. In most cases, however, the one-volume *Summary Catalogue Index* is the one you will need to check first. Unless otherwise indicated, all references are to this volume.

There are a number of *Source Lists* in the National Archives of Scotland, on the Index Room shelves, on a wide range of topics – emigration, Highlands and Islands, education, etc. These indicate where in the holdings of the NAS (not elsewhere) you may find documents dealing with each subject. *A Military Source List* (two volumes) – indexed by regiment, battle and campaign – and *List of American Documents* (indexed) have been published. The other lists are useful but take time to scan as they are arranged by class of record in which the reference is found – not by person, place or event – and they are not indexed.

The system is confusing at first but once you spend a little time in the record office, you will get used to it. *Tracing Your Ancestors in the Scottish Record Office* by Cecil Sinclair is a useful guide both to content of the various classes of records and how to access them.

FINDING YOUR WAY ROUND THE NAS

While waiting for documents you have ordered to be brought to your desk, your time will be well spent in browsing through the catalogues, finding out what is available and how the system works.

---

7 CHURCH RECORDS

The Old Parish Registers are an integral part of the records of the Church of Scotland and by law have been entrusted into the keeping of the Registrar General in New Register House – but there is a wealth of other material relating to the work of the church which is of value to the family historian in both providing genealogical information and putting 'flesh on the bones' of ancestors. There has been no statutory directive as to where these records should be housed. Many are in the National Archives of Scotland, others are in local archives (the NAS have retransmitted many to the relevant local archives) and some are still in the parishes concerned.

To find out what church records for the parish are held in the NAS, consult the CH2 catalogue under the name of the parish in which you are interested: the records for each congregation are given a number. Next look up the CH2 repertory of records under that number to see what is contained in the holding. Order the items you wish to see by putting on your slip CH2 plus the number given to the congregation plus the number given to the particular volume or item. If a particular item on a repertory is marked 'M', you will be able to look at the record in the NAS on microfilm. Some retransmitted material has not been filmed and you will have to go to the archive concerned to view the records.

KIRK SESSION RECORDS

The kirk session, particularly in the later 16th, 17th and early 18th century, was perhaps the most important authority in local society and touched the lives of persons of all classes of society, but particularly of the ordinary people and the poor. The Church was responsible for the moral welfare of the parishioners but also had responsibilities for the schools and, until the Poor Law of 1845, for the care of the poor. Its work is reflected in the kirk session minutes which are a rich source of information about people and life of the past. Kirk session minutes are not indexed but often there are side-heads which make it quick and easy to find a particular case. It is always worth reading the kirk session minutes of a parish in which an ancestor lived to gain a vivid insight into the life of the parish at the time.

You may find in the minutes, accounts and other parish records:

- Disciplinary cases – for adultery, fornication, swearing, Sabbath-breaking, disruption of the peace and other matters. The offences were reported in detail and witnesses were called, sometimes relatives of the accused, and often described by occupation and age. In cases of illegitimacy, the woman was put under pressure to reveal the name of the father who was also summoned to appear before the session. The amount of cases heard depended on the enthusiasm of the elders and minister in a particular parish. As the 18th century went on, the authority of the church declined and there tend to be less disciplinary cases reported.

- Irregular marriage cases – which often became apparent when the first child was brought for baptism. The couple would be summoned and fined and an entry put in the minutes or accounts. Such entries may supply information lacking from the parish register.

- Testimonials required by anyone moving from one parish to another, attesting their good reputation. These may be in the form of individual slips of paper or they may be recorded in the kirk session minutes. Only some have survived.

- Lists of lairs or details of graves in the burial ground. Records of lairs and arguments over the rights to them sometime resulted in mini-genealogies as a lair might have been owned by one family for several generations. Lair books (particularly more modern ones) may still be held by the individual cemeteries run by the district councils.

- Pew rents – usually only lists of names and useful as 'sightings' – but sometimes disputes arose over rights to pews which could reveal several generations using the same pew. The poor might also have pews allocated to named persons.

- Lists of the poor – in either the accounts or with the minutes. These lists are rarely of genealogical value as they usually only record names without any description or designation and the payment made to each person by the Session. You may find some certificates of poverty which give full details of the circumstances of an individual claiming parish assistance. In some instances there were disputes between two parishes as to which was responsible for the care of a poor person: the case would be heard in the Sheriff Court and provide a great deal of information. After the passing of the Poor Law Act of 1845, the responsibility for care of the poor passed to the Parochial Boards which were then established.

- Parish listings – communion rolls, lists of young communicants, examination rolls, names of heads of households and other listings of inhabitants. Many of these listings – particularly communion rolls – belong to the 19th century but they can be informative in providing information pre-dating the 1841 census. Communion rolls often included names of adults, where they lived, occupations and – most importantly – dates of death or removal and sometimes details of emigration. Some of the listings go back to the 17th century – there are lists of families in part of Canongate, Edinburgh in 1661 and 1684, and an even earlier one for St Cuthberts, Edinburgh with a list of parishioners 1632–39. A later listing of inhabitants dated 1798 for the parish of St Cyrus named every person there, giving occupation, residence, relationships and indicating whether each family was episcopalian, seceder or belonged to the Church of Scotland. There are a few listings at the end of the 18th century at the time of the Napoleonic Wars relating to those in the parish capable of bearing arms, men who were liable to balloted for the militia.

HERITORS' RECORDS

The heritors were the local property owners who, together with the Church, had responsibilities for support of the poor, and upkeep of the school, the church and the manse. Most surviving records of the heritors are in the National Archives of Scotland (class HR). There is an appendix to the HR repertory noting where heritors' records are to be found with other records such as Gifts and Deposits. Some interesting cases may be found in the heritors' records concerning the poor, which give a great deal of information about the circumstances of the person concerned.

PRESBYTERY RECORDS

The presbytery – formed of a group of parishes – was the administrative body above the kirk session. To find out in which presbytery a particular parish was included, consult either the *First (Old)* or *Second (New) Statistical Account* for that parish where this information is given under the heading of the parish account. The *Fasti Ecclesiae Scoticanae*, edited by Hew Scott, is a valuable book of reference, giving biographical details of the careers of all ministers of the Church of Scotland since the Reformation; it also shows within which presbytery each parish came.

The presbytery was responsible for hearing cases referred to it by the kirk session – these might be concerned with more serious charges such as witchcraft or habitual offending. The kirk session minutes may state that a certain case will be referred to the presbytery and further information can then be found in the presbytery minutes. The minutes of the presbyteries are not indexed but if a case previously heard in the kirk session is to be presented there, an approximate date will be known, making searching quite easy.

The presbytery was also concerned with the supervision and examination of ministers, with the upkeep of the school and behaviour of the schoolmaster, and the care of the church and manse.

SYNOD RECORDS

The synod was the next up in the hierarchy of the church courts and administrative system. Some disciplinary cases were heard and the records contain some references to ministers and elders but these records are less likely to be of value to the family historian.

GENERAL ASSEMBLY RECORDS

The General Assembly was the highest church court and was widely involved in appointing ministers, in morality and in education.

Cases of vacancies in parishes when there was a dispute over the appointment of a minister involved votes being taken by those for and against the candidates and resulted in long lists of heads of households. A great many such cases were heard, particularly in the first half of the 18th century. These lists provide valuable 'sightings' of individuals. The CH1 volumes are not indexed but are catalogued chronologically. Reference to the *Fasti Ecclesiae Scoticanae* will show when a minister died or moved to another parish and it may be worth checking the CH1 volumes at that time to see if a disputed vacancy followed.

The General Assembly also dealt with some matrimonial matters, the conduct of ministers, supply of ministers overseas and Royal Bounty Committee papers, concerned with the administration of money for the Reformation of the Highlands and Islands, providing for itinerant preachers and catechists in the area.

DISSENTING CHURCH RECORDS

The organisation of dissenting churches – Relief Church, Free Church, etc. – was similar to the Church of Scotland's, with kirk sessions, presbyteries, synods and sometimes a general assembly. If the family you are seeking might have belonged to such a church, consult the CH3 repertory, or look for records in a local archive.

8 TESTAMENTS, DISPOSITIONS & SETTLEMENTS

Though relatively few people left a testament, disposition or settlement, a number did – of all classes of society, both men and women – and these documents are a valuable source of information, both in terms of genealogy and in throwing light on how people in the past lived.

The following sections will provide a guide to finding and using testamentary material in the records of the Commissary Court and of the Sheriff Court and other courts.

THE COMMISSARY COURTS (UP TO C. 1823)

Up until about 1823, the Commissary Courts were responsible for registering testaments and the records of these are held in the National Archives of Scotland.

The courts of the Commissaries – or of the Officials as they were sometimes called – were established before the Reformation and had wide powers in matters claimed by the Church to come within their jurisdiction: the appointment of executors, confirmation of testaments, administration in cases of intestacy, divorce, legitimacy, marriage, actions for slander and all contracts or obligations made under oath. In 1560 – at the time of the Reformation – the Commissary Courts were abolished but in 1563 were reconstituted as civil courts which dealt with much the same matters as the pre-Reformation courts. Circa 1823 (there is an overlap in some areas), the business of the Commissary Courts was transferred to the Sheriff Courts.

Registers of Testaments

In Scotland the word 'testament' was used in two ways:

- The confirmation of an executor appointed in a case of intestacy – known as a 'testament dative'
- The confirmation of the executors appointed by the deceased himself in his latterwill – known as a 'testament testamentar'.

In both cases the property conveyed – in the testament dative or testament testamentar – was only the moveable property such as farm stock, money, furniture, or implements. Land was regarded as heritable property. In some cases, a testament dative was registered by a creditor who was appointed as the executor *qua creditor*. An inventory of the deceased's moveable goods and gear was then made so that the creditor might be paid what he was owed.

Very occasionally a testament dative is recorded for someone who died testate leaving a trust, disposition or settlement but who did not in that document appoint an executor. The commissary was then responsible for confirming the appointment of an executor after the death of the person.

A testament testamentar is likely to be of much greater value than a testament dative, and to include more genealogical detail, but a testament dative should never be underestimated: in most cases some members of the family are named and information about date of death, occupation and residence may be included.

SCAN is creating an index to all testaments recorded from the early 1500s up to 1875. The indexes will be searchable electronically on the network under person, place, occupation and date, for the whole of Scotland. Images of the testaments or wills will be digitised and the image, linked to the index entry, will be available on-line. Copies of the documents will be available on payment of a fee. For progress on this project, consult their website http://www.scan.org.uk. When looking for a testament using paper indexes, it is first necessary to find out which Commissary Court had jurisdiction over a particular parish. The jurisdiction of the Commissary Courts was based on the bounds of the pre-Reformation bishoprics and therefore does not always follow the boundaries of the sheriffdoms.

Check the list of parishes, page 218 onwards. In some cases, it may be wise to search the indexes to the registers of testaments of adjoining commissariots. The date of commencement of the registers for the various Commissary Courts varies considerably –

EDINBURGH COMMISSARY COURT

Edinburgh Commissary Court was the 'head' court and could confirm the testament of a person living anywhere in Scotland – as well as being the court where a testament concerning the moveable property of anyone living outwith Scotland was confirmed. It is always wise to check the Indexes to Testaments recorded in Edinburgh Commissary Court, in addition to that of the local Commissary Court.

the earliest being Edinburgh commencing in 1514 – but many registers have been lost or destroyed.

Indexes to the Registers of Testaments

There are printed indexes, published by the Scottish Record Society, to surviving registers of testaments in all the Commissary Courts up to 1800. The date given in the index is the date of registration – which could be a considerable time – perhaps several years – after the death of the person concerned. In some cases more than one testament was recorded, the later ones being known as 'eiks' usually referring to items which were not included in the inventories. It is always worth consulting these, as well as the main testament. The index often includes details of occupation or residence of the deceased person, which make it easier to identify a relevant entry. Women are indexed under their maiden names but there is a cross-reference to the entry under their husband's name – for example, 'John Leslie – see Strachan, Marjorie'. The index does not indicate whether it is a testament dative or a testament testamentar (which contains a latterwill) but both may contain useful information.

The printed indexes are available in the National Archives of Scotland, but will also be found in many libraries and archives. The bound volumes of indexes usually contain indexes to several commissariots. The Edinburgh Testaments are contained in three volumes. The existence of indexes makes searching for a relevant testament both quick and easy.

From 1801 to about 1824 (the date when responsibility for confirming testaments officially passed to the Sheriff Courts varies a little from place to place) there are typed indexes to the registers of testaments in the National Archives of Scotland Index Room. For some of the courts there are separate indexes; the others are indexed together in one volume which indicates in which Commissary Court the testament was registered, as follows:

- Edinburgh Commissary Court Index – 1801–29
- Glasgow Commissary Court Index – 1801–23
- Inverness Commissary Court Index – 1820–24
- Orkney Commissary Court – Confirmations 1806–23: Inventories 1809–31
- Peebles Commissary Court Index – 1801–27
- St. Andrews Commissary Court Index – 1801–23
- Wigtown Commissary Court – 1811–26
- General Index for all the other Commissary Courts 1801 up to 1829 (the terminal date varies).

When you have found an entry in an index (either printed or manuscript) which is of interest, find the CC (Commissary Court) number given to the relevant court (CC1-22) in the Parish List on page 218. There is a two-volume repertory of the records of the Commissary Courts arranged by CC number in the Index Room of the National Archives of Scotland. The first page of the part dealing with each court lists all the records of that court. Find the number of the section titled 'Register of Testaments' and turn to the detailed list of the volumes in that section. Note the number given to the volume which covers the date of the testament you have picked out in the index.

EXAMPLE

The index to the commissariot of Brechin shows that Robert Findlay, shipmaster in Dundee had a testament registered on 7 December 1765. The Commissary Court records for Brechin are listed under CC3: Section 3 concerns the Register of Testaments: volume 11 covers the date 7 December 1765. Your order slip, therefore, would have on it: CC3/3/11.

The manuscript indexes give a page number but unfortunately the printed indexes do not. A few volumes have a contents list at the beginning or end: in some there are side-heads which show the date and the name of the defunct: in others you have to look for the date of registration which is **either in the last paragraph or at the end of the last paragraph but one**. The testaments are usually copied into the register in chronological order – though there are some exceptions.

Content of a Testament

You may sometimes have problems in reading a testament so it is important to know the form of the document to enable you to pick out the parts that are likely to contain the most information.

- The first paragraph in both a testament dative and a testament testamentar states the name of the deceased person, often their residence or occupation or both, and sometimes the date (or approximate date) of death. The name of the executor is then given and often details of his or her relationship to the defunct – or the creditor who acts as the executor is described as 'qua creditor'.

- The next section concerns the inventory of the moveable estate of the deceased, with each item valued. The total – 'summa' – is then given. This part of a testament – often detailing farm stock, crops sown, household furnishings and even items of a wardrobe – is interesting in throwing light on the background of the family. As the testament is only concerned with 'moveable' goods – not with land termed as heritable property – even well-to-do families may appear to be worth little.

- Then follows the debts owed to the defunct – 'debts owing in'. Sometimes members of the family are included in the list.

- Debts 'owing out' are next itemised, and again may include relations. Money may be due to a landlord or feudal superior – a useful name to note as it may provide a lead to finding rentals.

- The net value of the estate is estimated and the commissary notes his 'quot' – the tax due. There is then a line which states 'to be divided in two parts' or ' to be divided in three parts ' or 'no division'.

- In the case of a testament testamentar, the 'latterwill' follows – also known as the 'legacie'. This was written during the lifetime of the person concerned who usually nominated his executors and recorded any personal wishes as to the disposition of his goods and gear. This section often contains a great deal of genealogical information.

- The final two paragraphs concern the confirmation of the testament by the commissary officer and usually the naming of a 'cautioner' responsible for seeing that the executor carried out his duties properly. The cautioner was often a close relative.

Edicts, Petitions & Processes

The registers of testaments are the most commonly used records of the Commissary Courts but if you look at the repertory of the records of each Commissary Court (on the first page of the CC repertory for that particular Commissary Court) you will see that

---

DIVISION OF MOVEABLE PROPERTY

Under Scots law, the divisions of moveable property were:

- If the dead person was survived by a spouse and child or children, the net value of the moveable estate was divided in three – one part to the spouse, one to be divided among the children equally (excepting the eldest son if he inherited heritable property), and the third part was 'free' – and could be left according to the wishes of the defunct if he expressed them. If he did not, then that share was divided in two and half added to each of the other two portions.

- If the defunct was survived only by a spouse or by child/children, then the net value of the moveable estate was divided in two – one half being 'free', the other half going to the spouse or children.

- If there is no division, this indicates that the deceased was not survived by either a spouse or child or children.

A testament may not always mention all members of the family and the 'division' can therefore be of value in indicating whether there were surviving children or a spouse. The eldest son was often not named in a testament, as in cases of intestacy he did not share in the moveable estate if he was the heir to the heritable property.

---

there are a number of other classes of records – including processes, warrants of testaments, registers of inventories, petitions, edicts and deeds. The number of surviving records does vary from court to court.

Warrant This was the draft of a testament and in some instances the warrant has survived when a register of testaments has been lost. Warrants are bound in bundles according to date. If the register of testaments is deficient for the Commissary Court in which you are interested, it may be worth checking the warrants if you have an approximate date of death – but remember that the testament might be recorded some time after the death occurred.

Edicts of executry These were writs issued by the commissaries requesting any person or persons who had an interest in the moveable goods of a deceased person to come forward to be confirmed as executors. A great many of these edicts have survived, often in cases when no testament is extant. The edict may contain as much genealogical information as a testament dative – stating the name of the executor and relationship to the defunct whose name, occupation, place of residence and date of death may also be given. The amount of detail varies. Sometimes there were disputes over the appointment of an executor and such cases provide a great deal of information. Even when someone was appointed executor dative qua creditor, the edict may contain interesting details about the circumstances of the deceased.

Edicts of tutory or curatory These were issued in the case of children under 21 whose father had died or when someone was unable to manage their own affairs. A tutor was appointed for boys under the age of 14 and for girls under the age of 12. After that, until the child was 'of full age' – 21 – a curator could be chosen by the minor to take over this charge. A tutor might be chosen by a parent during his or her lifetime, but in cases of intestacy, the commissary officer made the appointment – usually the nearest relatives on the father's and mother's sides. The information given is therefore of genealogical value. These edicts are sometimes found intermingled with the other edicts, but there may be separate bundles of curatorial and tutorial inventories.

Inventories Taking an inventory of the moveable goods of the dead person's estate was one of the first tasks of the executor and of the tutor. This forms part of a registered testament but you may find warrants of inventories which are additional to those recorded with the testaments – or registers of inventories when there is no register of testaments. Inventories are also sometimes found attached to edicts – often referring to claims for the cost of

---

INDEXES TO THE RECORDS OF THE COMMISSARY COURTS

Check the repertory for the Commissary Court in which you are interested. For most courts there is a section titled 'Inventories of Records'. This is a list (not an index) of various classes of documents – edicts, processes, etc. – usually arranged chronologically which makes it possible to pick out records of likely interest.

All the records of Argyll Commissary Court from 1700–1825 are now catalogued and indexed; a typescript copy of the index is in the National Archives of Scotland.

providing for the funeral. Others will detail every moveable within a house, from furniture to clothing. The inventories, as well as being of considerable interest from the point of view of the social background of the person concerned, may include genealogical information.

Petitions These were sometimes made to the commissary officer by the executors and usually concerned financial matters, for example, requests that they be allowed to collect debts due to the deceased, to roup his effects to raise money or have access to the belongings and documents of the deceased. These papers often contain quite a lot of information about the family and its affairs.

Processes These were the documents relating to cases heard in the Commissary Courts. A great many were concerned with slander, and the recovery of debts, some of which concerned the estates of deceased persons. Processes are a valuable source both of social history and of genealogical information.

THE SHERIFF COURTS – COMMISSARY BUSINESS

Following the Commissary Courts (Scotland) Act of 1823, the Sheriff Courts became responsible for the business previously undertaken in the Commissary Courts – the confirmation of executors, and the registering of inventories and wills (also referred to as trust dispositions, settlements or testamentary deeds). There was however an overlap in the transfer of responsibilities and between 1823 and 1829 it may be wise to check both the records of the relevant Commissary Court and of the Sheriff Court which took over its duties.

Edinburgh Sheriff Court dealt with all testamentary business of anyone dying outwith Scotland but leaving moveable property in Scotland. There is a separate volume for Edinburgh Sheriff Court commissary records titled *Edinburgh Commissary Office – SC70*. For the period 1858–1900 in the case of someone dying in England or Ireland, there is a volume titled *Probates Resealed* – an index to English and Irish probates. The index gives a date which is then checked in SC70/6 to find the relevant volume number to be ordered up.

The first step is to identify the relevant Sheriff Court. Up till 1974 the administrative divisions of Scotland were the counties. In most counties there was one Sheriff Court but in some there was more than one. The Sheriff Courts were sometimes referred to by the county name and sometimes by the name of the town where the Sheriff Court was situated. Another complication is

THE OLD COUNTY NAMES

Some of the counties changed their names and it is important to remember that:

- Forfarshire = Angus
- Edinburghshire = Midlothian
- Haddingtonshire = East Lothian
- Linlithgowshire = West Lothian
- Elgin = Moray
- Zetland = Orkney & Shetland

that where there was more than one sheriffdom within a county, not all these Sheriff Courts handled commissary business.

The parish list on page 218 will show in which sheriffdom the parish in which you are interested is situated. In the second half of the 19th century, some additional courts were appointed to handle commissary business. From 1876 onwards, the Confirmations will indicate in what court the inventory and will were recorded.

Indexes to Personal Estates of Defuncts in the Sheriff Courts c.1823–75

Prior to 1823, the registers of testaments are the class of records which are indexed. From 1823 onwards, you need to look for 'Inventories' or 'Personal Estates of Defuncts'. There are searching aids for these records in each Sheriff Court, either as printed or manuscript lists of contents or indexes.

The following counties and years are covered by the printed indexes, each volume covering several counties:

- Edinburgh, Haddington, Linlithgow   1827–45, 1846–65
- Aberdeen, Kincardine, Banff, Elgin, Nairn, Inverness, Ross, Cromarty, Sutherland, Caithness, Orkney, Shetland   1846–67
- Fife, Dundee, Forfar, Perth, Clackmannan, Kinross, Stirling   1846–67
- Argyll, Bute, Dunbarton, Lanark, Renfrew   1846–67
- Ayr, Kirkcudbright, Wigtown, Dumfries, Roxburgh, Berwick, Peebles, Selkirk   1846–67

The printed indexes of Personal Estates of Defuncts (on the shelves of the NAS Index Room and available in other libraries) give the name of the deceased person, the date of death, the Sheriff Court and year in which the inventory is registered, and usually some details such as place of residence or occupation. The year of registration is written in a shortened form: '29' = 1829 or '48' = 1848. Women are listed after men. There is a letter against each entry showing whether the person died testate or intestate:

- The letters D, F, or H indicate intestacy
- The letters C, E, or G indicate testacy
- The letters A and B do not indicate either testacy or intestacy.

For years when there is no printed index, find the repertory of the relevant Sheriff Court in the NAS Index Room and next to it there will be one or more volumes with blue labels titled 'Inventories'. These are either manuscript contents lists (in chronological order) or indexes (usually arranged alphabetically in blocks of years) of persons for whom inventories were recorded from c. 1823 onwards (in most cases including the years covered by the printed indexes). The contents lists and indexes give the name of the person, the year in which the inventory is recorded, a volume number and page number. It will often not tell you whether the person died testate or intestate. Even if you find an entry in the printed index, it may be worth checking it in the manuscript index as there is the bonus of a volume number and page number.

Consult the section of the relevant Sheriff Court repertory headed 'Commissary' or 'Commissary Court' and then find the

---

EXAMPLE

For someone whose inventory was recorded in Banff Sheriff Court on 20 November 1862, you would put down on an order slip SC2/40/20 – SC2 for the number given to Banff Sheriff Court, followed by 40 – the number given to the register of confirmations, inventories and wills, followed by 20 – the volume covering the dates 19 November 1862–15 September 1864.

'Register of confirmations, inventories and wills' (the wording may vary slightly). In some Sheriff Courts the wills are separate. Find the volume which covers the date given in the index.

If you have consulted a manuscript index or contents list which gives the volume number, it is important to recheck this reference against the Sheriff Court commissary repertory as some of the records have been renumbered since the manuscript indexes were made.

The Inventory

An inventory will give you the name of the deceased, his date of death and possibly include details of where he lived and what he did. There will also be a statement as to whether he/she died testate or intestate. The name of the executor follows and the inventory of the deceased's moveable goods.

If it was a case of testacy, then the inventory will state in what court the will is registered. In some cases (as in Banff) the will is included in the same register as the inventory and will be quoted immediately after the inventory. In many other courts, however, the will is registered separately. It could be recorded in the same Sheriff Court in a register of wills or testaments, in the Books of Council and Session or in a burgh register of deeds. (See page 141 for further information on the registers of deeds.) The date of recording this document should be shortly before or on the same as the date of the inventory.

Calendar of Confirmations and Inventories after 1875

From 1876 onwards there are annual printed volumes of indexes to the confirmation of executries, covering the whole of Scotland. Women are indexed under their married names. These can be consulted in the Historical Search Room in the National Archives of Scotland up to 1929 and after that date in the Legal Search Room in the same building. The list of more recent confirmations can be consulted on fiche. A confirmation may be registered soon

---

ORDERING UP TESTAMENTS AND INVENTORIES

Original volumes of testaments are now withdrawn but microfilm copies of most registers can be consulted in the NAS or in Mormon libraries world-wide. Other Commissary Court records (such as edicts, processes, etc.) will probably need to be ordered up two days in advance.

Most of the Sheriff Court records – inventories, wills, and deeds – are out-housed and have to be ordered up two days in advance.

after the death or some years later – it is important to search on for several years after the known date of death.

A confirmation will state the date of registration of the executry, tell you when the deceased died, give an address and usually an occupation, name the executors and include the net value of the moveable estate. It will also state whether the deceased died intestate or testate and in the latter case, in what court the will was registered. You can then locate the will in the relevant court records, taking the date as that of the confirmation or a little earlier. The inventory and will had to be recorded before they could be confirmed.

TRUSTS, DISPOSITIONS & SETTLEMENTS

Many people – particularly those in the better-off classes of society such as merchants and landowners, but also sometimes craftsmen and farmers – recorded a 'will' in a register of deeds, the document usually being described as a trust, disposition, mutual disposition and settlement or deed of settlement. The person drawing up the deed normally appointed executors and if there was a possibility that the children might still be minors when the father died, tutors were named to look after their affairs until they reached the age when they could chose their own curators.

A testamentary deed often contains a great deal of information of value both genealogically and in filling in the social background of the family. It may deal with the disposal not only of moveable goods but of the heritable property (land and houses) as well. Bequests may be made to many members of the family and other relatives.

COURTS REGISTERING DEEDS

A deed could be recorded in any court competent to register such documents. It might therefore be found in:

- The Register of Deeds (also known as the Books of Council and Session)
- A Sheriff Court Register of Deeds
- A Burgh Court Register of Deeds
- A Commissary Court Register of Deeds
- A Franchise Court Register of Deeds (not Barony)

If there is a gap in a particular register of deeds, it is possible that warrants may fill the gap. Detailed information on the registers of deeds is given on page 141. Prior to the 18th century, deeds may also be found in the Protocol Books of the notaries.

9 LANDLORD & TENANT

Not everyone owned land but the possession of land was more widely spread than is sometimes believed and persons of many classes of society are represented. In the case of farmers, it is often not known whether an ancestor was a tenant or proprietor of the land and research must be undertaken to establish this – and, in the case of tenancy, to discover the name of the landlord. Records concerning the administration of an estate may throw light on the family and life of an ancestor whether as tenant or as labourer, with rentals, leases, payments to workers on the estate and details of day-to-day management of the lands.

LAND OWNERSHIP

Land ownership in Scotland was based on the feudal system. This involved two kinds of interest in land: the superiority and the property itself. Most land was deemed to belong to the Crown who as the *superior* then granted it heritably to a vassal on certain terms, originally often in return for military service but later usually on payment of nominal rents, giving the vassal a feu charter to these lands. The vassal could then *sub-infeudate* these lands (again granting the lands heritably under a charter) to another vassal, the granter then becoming the immediate *subject superior* over this new owner of the feu. In the royal burghs, the burgage lands were held directly of the Crown under the terms of the burgh charter. The charter was accompanied by – or later had incorporated in it – the precept, which was the authority for sasine to be given, the sasine concluding the transaction and being the legal registration of ownership of a feu or of land.

Property could also be sold (other terms used are 'dispone' or 'alienate'), mortgaged under a wadset as security for a loan or the lands could be inherited by an heir. In such cases the new possessor of the property became bound to the feudal superior from whom the previous owner held the lands. The sale, inheritance or wadset was then recorded in a register of sasines.

Register of the Great Seal

Charters – which set out the terms under which land was to be held from the superior – are not a source which is likely to have a first claim on the attention of most researchers, but for those who may have had ancestors who held lands from the Crown in the 17th century or earlier, the *Register of the Great Seal* is an easily accessible source and contains references to a great many persons, both small lairds and great landowners.

This register covered grants to vassals, and confirmation of grants made by the vassals to their subject-vassals. There are printed abridgements contained in eleven volumes entitled *Register of the Great Seal of Scotland* (or *Registrum Magni Sigilli Regum Scotorum*) for the years 1314–1668 (written in Latin up to 1651). It is usually (though not always) sufficient to search the printed abridgements, to avoid the labour of reading a lengthy Latin document.

The printed volumes are indexed by person (including all the main persons mentioned in each charter) and by place. The *Register of the Great Seal* comes under Chancery (class reference C in the National Archives of Scotland). The printed abridgements are widely available in libraries and archives in Scotland and elsewhere. After 1668, there are only typed indexes – not abridgements – in the NAS referring to the person receiving the charter.

In some cases a first draft of a Crown Charter has survived in the *Register of Signatures*. These are written in English. To see what has survived, check the Index to Signatures (National Archives of Scotland reference SIG).

From 1617 onwards, when the main series of registers of sasines commenced, it is usually easier to consult a sasine than to look for the charter.

Charters & Family Papers

There are several collections of early charters in the National Archives of Scotland and the 15-volume *Calendar of Charters* covering the period 1142–1600 is indexed.

Charters and other documents concerning land ownership will often be found in family muniments (some of which have been published). There are many collections of family papers in the National Archives of Scotland, in the section called Gifts and Deposits (class reference GD). Check the *Summary Catalogue* under the name (or title) of the family concerned. If a deposit has been made in the NAS, then there will be a GD reference. Those with a reference GD1 plus a number are small collections: GD2 onwards are larger deposits. Go to the shelves in the Index Room holding the individual GD catalogues arranged by GD reference number. These will give details of what is contained in each collection and give the reference for ordering out a volume, bundle or individual document. This will be the relevant GD number plus the number given to the section, box or bundle. The contents of most muniments are arranged in subject sections and there is often one which contains 'titles' or 'writs' or which will refer to records of land ownership. If you can find a bundle titled 'Progress of Writs', this may contain copies of sasines or a catalogue which may enable you to trace back ownership of the lands over several centuries.

Most archives and some national and local libraries also hold collections of family papers. Many of these are itemised in the Scottish Record Association *Archival Summaries*. A number of collections of family papers have been printed by various clubs and societies. *Scottish Texts and Calendars – an Analytical Guide to Serial Publications*, published by the Scottish History Society, gives a list of these.

Sasines

An instrument of sasine is the document completing the act of conveyance, though in the period before registers of sasines were introduced, in many cases the charter survived but the sasine did not.

There are four main types of transactions concerning the transfer of land:

- Inheritance
- Purchase
- Transfer from one person to another as security for a loan (a wadset) and redemption (repayment) of the loan
- Re-registration of ownership of land – often done when a couple marry and a wife is given joint infeftment.

THE VALUE OF SASINES

From the point of view of the genealogist, sasines concerning inheritance are the most useful, but others dealing with the acquisition of property and lending or borrowing money on the security of land may throw a great deal of light on a family and its business transactions, as well as mentioning other members of the family and providing addresses which – after 1840 – can be checked in census returns.

Leases were not recorded in a register of sasines.

In each case, proof of possession was given by the handing over in the presence of witnesses a symbol of ownership such as earth and stone of the lands concerned, clap and happer of a mill, or coble for the fishings, and the written legal proof of the completion of the transaction in the form of an *instrument of sasine*. Procedures changed little until the second half of the 19th century.

PROTOCOL BOOKS

The earliest registers of the ownership of lands were kept by the notaries public – lawyers who were officially authorised to record legal documents of various kinds including sasines. Their protocol books were sometimes concerned with transactions taking place over several counties but might be more localised. Many of the royal burghs had their own notaries who kept protocol books. A few surviving protocol books go back to the end of the 15th century and there are a number which date to the 16th century, but many have been lost. The largest collection of protocol books is in the National Archives of Scotland (class NP) and there is a list at the beginning of the repertory detailing the main geographical areas covered by each notary, the dates for each book and whether it has been published. The protocol books of some of the royal burghs – including Aberdeen, Dundee, Glasgow and Stirling – are held in local archives and some are in repositories such as the National Library of Scotland.

Many protocol books are written in Latin and may be very difficult to read. Some have been transcribed, printed and indexed by societies such as the Scottish Record Society. A high degree of dedication and expertise is needed to tackle those which have not been printed.

REGISTERS OF SASINES – SECRETARY'S REGISTER, GENERAL & PARTICULAR REGISTERS

By the 17th century it was found that the system of recording sasines by the notaries was not satisfactory since the reputation of many was not above suspicion and the books were not always handed in. The first attempt to provide a national system of land registration was made in 1599 with the introduction of the Secretary's Register. Scotland was divided into 17 recording districts with a secretary appointed for each to keep a register of sasines. Not all the registers have survived and the system was abolished in 1609. Those that have survived in whole or in part are for Aberdeenshire, Kincardineshire, Ayrshire and the Bailiaries of Kyle, Carrick and Cunningham, Banffshire, Edinburgh and the Constabulary of Haddington, Linlithgow and Bathgate, Fife and Kinross, Inverness-shire, Ross-shire, Sutherland and Cromarty and Perthshire.

In 1617 the General Register of Sasines and the Particular Register of Sasines were instituted:

- The General Register of Sasines covered the whole of Scotland and any sasine could be registered there – but it was often used in the case of a transfer of property concerning an estate in which pieces of land were situated in various counties.

- The Particular Register of Sasines covered individual counties or specific parts of Scotland.

- The Royal Burghs kept their own Burgh Registers of Sasines – officially established in 1681, but a number of burgh registers of sasines go back before this date.

In 1868 the system was simplified and all sasines were kept on a county basis. In theory every transaction concerning the change of ownership of land should be registered in a sasine register but there are imperfections in the system. Sometimes – in cases of inheritance – an heir might not complete all the steps to taking up legal possession of his heritable property. Sometimes a registered deed may stand for a sasine as proof of ownership – and there may be problems in finding in which register, General, Particular or Burgh, a sasine is recorded. On the other hand the existence of a legal system of land registration going back to 1617 does offer great scope for tracing the ownership of property over this period.

All the General and Particular Sasines Registers are kept in the National Archives of Scotland. RS1-3 is the class reference number for the General Registers of Sasines, while the class reference given to the various Particular Registers of Sasines can be found in the RS repertory.

BURGH REGISTERS OF SASINES

It was one of the rights of royal burghs to keep a register of sasines for lands within their bounds. To find out if a town was erected as a royal burgh, consult *The Burghs of Scotland – A Critical List* by George Smith Pryde. The date of starting the register in each burgh varied widely and they were discontinued between 1926 and 1963. Most of these burgh registers of sasines are in the National Archives of Scotland but some, including some early ones for Glasgow, Aberdeen and Dundee are in the local archives.

There are few searching aids, though some of the burgh registers have typescript indexes after 1809. Lacking indexes, check the repertory of the particular burgh for minute books. As the sasines are concerned with a relatively small local area, it does not take too long to look through an unindexed volume of sasines.

SEARCHING AIDS – SASINES 1599–1780

Indexing is unfortunately sporadic. If there are no indexes, then look for minute books in the RS repertory. These are often quite informative: they are arranged in chronological order according to the date of registration, and sometimes include details of the lands conveyed, name of granter and grantee and terms under which the lands were given. Having found an entry for which you wish to study the full text, order up the required volume of sasines which includes the relevant date.

Where they exist, the indexes are also quite detailed, giving some description of the person concerned: occupation, place of residence and sometimes relationship – 'daughter of', 'son of', for example. The names of the granter and grantee are included as well as any-

---

ORDERING UP A SASINE: AN EXAMPLE

Searching for information on Andrew Reid, a tailor in Douglas, Lanarkshire in the 1770s.

Entry found in the Index to Lanarkshire Sasines 1721–80 (printed index):

Andrew Reid, tailor, Douglas, XXI. 176. His spouse, see Harkness, Jean.

Next entry: Andrew, son of Andrew R., tailor, Douglas, XXI.176.

The index entries therefore have already supplied some valuable genealogical information.

A check on the RS (Register of Sasines) number given to Lanarkshire shows that RS42 covers sasines recorded there from 1721 to 1780.

The order slip to be handed to the messenger in the Search Room should therefore have on it:

RS42/21. (You do not need to put on the folio number).

---

one else mentioned in the sasine as having a heritable right to the lands concerned. Names of tenants and witnesses are not included.

The sasine indexes will give a volume number and a folio number. You will then need to find the relevant RS number in the RS repertory.

The General Register of Sasines is indexed by person from 1617–1720. In the unindexed period – 1721–80 – minute books must be searched.

The table opposite gives details of the Particular Registers of Sasines which are indexed between 1617 and 1781 and includes reference to the Secretary's Register if it is extant.

REGISTERS	INDEXES
Aberdeen	1599–1609; 1617–60
Argyll, Dumbarton, Arran, Bute & Tarbert	1617–1780
Ayr, Kyle, Carrick and Cunningham	1599–1609; 1617–60
Banff	1600–09; 1617–1780
Berwick & Lauderdale	1617–1780
Caithness	Up to 1644, with Inverness; 1646–1780
Dumfries, Kirkcudbright & Annandale	1617–1780
Edinburgh, Haddington	1599–1609; 1617–60; 1741–80
Elgin, Forres & Nairn	1617–1780
Fife & Kinross	1603–09; 1617–60
Forfar	1620–1780
Inverness, Ross, Sutherland, Cromarty	1606–08; 1617–1780
Kincardine	1600–08; 1617–57
Kinross	Up to 1685, with Fife
Lanark (for Glasgow see Renfrew)	1618–1780
Orkney & Shetland	1617–60
Perth	1601–09
Renfrew & Barony of Glasgow	No indexes
Roxburgh, Selkirk & Peebles	No indexes
Stirling, Clackmannan & Menteith	No indexes
West Lothian	Up to 1760, with Edinburgh; 1700–60
Wigtown	No indexes

A sasine may be recorded in either the General or Particular Register of Sasines. If you do not find the sasine in which you are interested in the Particular Register, consult the General Register.

SEARCHING AIDS – 1781 ONWARDS: THE ABRIDGEMENTS

From 1781 onwards, searching the sasines becomes very much easier as they are all arranged on a county basis and there are printed abridgements. The LDS libraries may hold filmed copies of the abridgements for the years 1781–1868.

There are manuscript or printed indexes to the abridgements in the National Archives of Scotland. These with the volumes of printed abridgements are on open shelves in the stairwell below the stairs leading up to the Historical Reading Room. The indexes are arranged:

- By Person from 1781 to the present
- By Place from 1781–1830: from 1872 to the present

As with the earlier indexes, the Indexes to Persons include names of granter, grantee and of anyone else having a heritable interest in the property.

The Indexes to Places can be very useful as a contemporary gazetteer as they include most of the place-names mentioned in the abridgements – farms, townships, villages and areas of land, showing contemporary spellings.

The indexes and the abridgements are arranged by county, alphabetically round the stairwell, according to the modern names of the counties, but you will find that the old names of the counties are on the backs of the volumes: Forfarshire for Angus,

Edinburghshire for Midlothian, Haddingtonshire for East
Lothian, Linlithgowshire for West Lothian and Zetland for
Orkney and Shetland.

The earlier indexes are arranged in blocks of years, the later
ones are covered year by year. To consult a sasine in which you are
interested, find the volume of indexes and abridgements for the
county in which you think the property was situated and look at
the index for persons or places for the chosen period of years.
Against the index entry will be a number (or series of numbers).
Note the numbers and then look at the volume of abridgements
which covers the right period of years (it is important to check
this). Each abridgement has a number in brackets on the left-
hand side by the date of registration which is the number given in
the index. At the end of the abridgement is a reference which will
enable you to order up the full text of the sasine. This will be
either PR or GR followed by two sets of numbers. PR stands for
Particular Register of Sasines (for the county in which you are
searching) or GR for General Register of Sasines. The first set of
numbers refers to the volume number and the second to the page
number in the volume. On returning to the Historical Reading
Room to order up the sasine, go to the RS repertory (or there is a
chart on the wall in the Index Room) to find out the RS number
given to the particular county for the period after 1780, following
the same system as in the example already quoted.

In most cases, the information given in the abridgement will be
sufficient, but sometimes it is advisable to consult the full text of
the sasine. This may make it easier to understand what is happening in the transaction and there may be additional details.

UNDERSTANDING THE ABRIDGEMENTS

It is not always easy at first to understand the content of an abridgement. The following notes may help:

- If the abridgement contains the words 'registers disposition', 'gets disposition by' or 'gets assignation by' it is probable that property is changing hands consequent on a sale. 'Gets notarial instrument on disposition', or property given under 'a letter of heritable alienation' also indicates the buying of property.

- The phrase 'registers special and/or general service' shows that this is a case of property being inherited (more information will be found in the section on Retours).

- When the word 'bond' occurs – often as 'bond and disposition', then a mortgage is involved, and someone is being given sasine of certain property as security for a loan of money. The person *lending* the money '*gets* Bond and Disposition for £....' by the borrower 'over' certain lands which are mortgaged till the loan is repaid.

- Another sasine is then recorded when the bond is repaid. This is indicated by the phrase that the lender 'grants discharge of bond and disposition for £...' to the borrower and the lender now declares the mortgaged property 'disburdened thereof'.

The table opposite gives a glossary of the shortened terms used in abridgements.

THE FORM OF A SASINE

Like many legal documents, a sasine is often long, not easy to understand and contains a great deal of repetition. Another prob-

GLOSSARY OF SHORTENED TERMS IN ABRIDGEMENTS

Assig. – assignation

Disch. – discharge

Disp. – disposition

Inter alia – among others

Not. Instrument – notarial instrument (legal document)

Pro indiviso – undivided

Qua – as

Ratif. – ratification

Sp. and Gen. Serv. – special and general service

lem is that most sasines in the General and Particular Registers up until the 18th century were written in Latin. Sasines registered in the Burgh Registers of Sasines were usually written in the vernacular and were simpler in form. The *Formulary of Old Scots Legal Documents* compiled by Peter Gouldesbrough includes examples of a wide range of Scottish legal documents including sasines; and if the document is in Latin, a translation is given.

Sasines follow a set form and a knowledge of what is contained in each section often makes it unnecessary to read the whole document. The following is an outline of the usual form of a sasine recorded in the general or a particular register:

- In the heading, the date of registration is given and often a short summary in English of the lands concerned and the name of the person receiving sasine (being infeft). The first paragraph then gives the date of writing the sasine (usually shortly before the date of registration), the names of the parties concerned in the transaction and a description of the lands being conveyed.

- Three parties then 'compear' (appear):
  ❑ the procurator (*actornatus* in the Latin) appearing for the person who is being given sasine or sometimes this person may appear personally
  ❑ the bailie (*ballivus*) representing the person who owns the land and is now passing it to someone else
  ❑ the notary public who is the officiating lawyer.

- The procurator has in hands the 'precept of sasine' which is read aloud. This is the authorisation granted by the feudal superior of the lands that sasine should be given and again the lands to be conveyed are described. If the precept is described as 'a precept of clare constat', then the person being seised has had to prove that he has the right to inherit (see Retours, page 131). In this section reference may be made to the fact that the lands are 'under reversion' showing that this is a case of a mortgage – on repayment of the loan, the lands will revert to the original owner, the lender then renouncing his rights to the property. The date of signing the precept is given – sometimes some considerable time before the registration of the sasine – and signed before witnesses. The names of witnesses should always be noted as sometimes they are relatives of one of the parties concerned.

- Having recited yet again the terms of the sasine and the lands involved, sasine is then given by the notary to the new owner – physically by the giving of earth and stone or other suitable symbols and by the registration of 'instruments' or legal documents. These proceedings are again witnessed, usually by a different set of witnesses whose names should be noted.

The most important parts of a sasine are:

- The description of the lands concerned, and the names of the giver and getter (in the first paragraph)
- The terms under which the lands are conveyed – by inheritance, purchase or as a security for a loan, also in the first paragraph
- The witnesses to the precept and the witnesses to the giving of sasine.

RETOURS

Retours – Services of Heirs

Under Scots law, the eldest son inherited the land on the death of the landowner, though a father might during his lifetime dispone the property to his eldest son, reserving a liferent to himself. After 1868, heritable property could be bequeathed but in cases of intestacy, the law of primogeniture applied until 1964. If a man died without surviving sons, but leaving several daughters, these inherited the property jointly and were known as heirs portioners.

An heir had to prove his right to inherit land by being 'retoured' or 'served heir'. Death of an owner of property leaving an heir or other relative did not however always result in a retour as in many cases the new heir did not complete title for a long time.

The registers of retours provide a most useful source of information about landowners. A brieve was issued by Chancery instructing the local sheriff or burgh magistrates to empanel a jury and hold an inquest, to prove that the previous owner had full right to the lands and that the claimant to the lands was 'the nearest and lawful heir'. The official then returned – or retoured – a verdict to Chancery, which was the authority for infefting (seising) the person in their heritable property. There are two kinds of retours:

- General retours covering the whole heritable property of the deceased person
- Special retours which were concerned with specified parts of the property.

Retours before 1700

Not all retours have survived but there is a summary of most of those which are extant, covering the period 1545–1699 in a three-volume printed edition entitled *Inquisitionum ad Capellam Regis Retornatarum Abbreviatio*. Volumes 1 and 2 contain the abstracts, written in Latin and arranged by county. Volume 3 contains indexes to persons and places (as they appear in the text) for the entries in the other volumes. The information given in the entry includes the name of the deceased person, the name of the heir, their relationship and in the case of 'Inquisitiones Speciales' a description of the lands inherited. A volume number is given which enables you to order up the original retour if required, in the Chancery records – C22. All retours are in Latin.

When looking for records relating to inheritance in the period 1264–1600, it may be worth looking through the indexes to the printed volumes of Exchequer Rolls as there are some references to money due to the crown for feudal casualties – such as relief, a tax payable to the Crown by the heir when he becomes the vassal of the superior on the death of his ancestor. After the fatal battle of Flodden in 1513 when so many Scots were killed, the Crown granted remission of many entry dues of their heirs.

Retours from 1700

From 1700 onwards, there are printed abstracts of retours in English arranged alphabetically by the name of the person who is inheriting. If the heir does not have the same surname as the person who has died, check the back of each volume of abstract retours where there is a index of the names of the persons who died. From 1700–1859 the indexes are printed in decennial blocks covering the whole of Scotland; from 1860 onwards there are annual indexes. The printed volumes are in the Index Room in the NAS in the section covering Chancery Records (class reference C). These indexes may also be available in other libraries or family history centres. The Scottish Genealogy Society sells CDs of both sets of Indexes to Retours (1544–1699 and 1700–1859).

In most cases the information given in the abstract is all that is of value to the genealogist: names of deceased and the heir, occupations, sometimes date of death and indication of the lands concerned; however, if a person is served heir to their uncle, grandfather – someone other than their parent – then the full text of the retour in many cases will spell out the relationship and list any intervening generations. It is sometimes possible to trace the outline history of a landed family back through a number of generations just by checking the indexes to Services of Heirs. Most of the entries refer to persons of some means, but there are a surprising number of 'ordinary' people who inherited property.

The original retours are in Latin up to 1847 but even with a small knowledge of Latin, it should be possible to find out what is happening. The class reference number of the original retours in the National Archives of Scotland is C22 up to 1847 and C28 thereafter. Note the date of registration of the retour given in the printed index and order up the volume which covers that date.

Some Sheriff Courts and some royal burghs have retours among their records. These may refer to the actual proceedings of holding the assize before retouring their findings and may be informative.

Register of Tailzies

Tailzies, or entails, are documents which set out the destination of heritage, ensuring that if the heir dies, then the next-in-line is named and setting out any conditions attached to the inheritance. In the case of a more remote heir or an heir through the female side of the family, this might involve taking the family name. Many tailzies are very detailed and provide a great deal of valuable information about various branches of the family. They might, therefore, be useful if there is a tradition that your ancestor was related to a well-known landed family.

The National Archives of Scotland class reference number is RT1. There is an index to the register for the years 1688–1833 (partly printed, partly in manuscript) arranged alphabetically under the family name, and then chronologically under that name if there is more than one tailzie. The index for the period after 1833 up to 1938 will be found in the Legal Search Room (on the ground floor of the National Archives of Scotland).

TENANTS & OCCUPIERS

It is often not certain whether a person owned property or leased it. From 1781 onwards, this information can be found by searching the abridgements to the registers of sasines. You can either search under the name of the person or if the name of the farm or property is known, consult the Index to Places (not available for the years 1830–70). This search has the advantage that a sasine registered for the conveyance of this property should name the proprietor, though care must be taken to study the sasine as the document may concern a mortgage rather than a disposition or record of inheritance.

From 1855 onwards, Valuation Rolls will state who is the proprietor, tenant and occupier of each property (see page 62).

Before 1781, acquiring information about tenant and proprietor is more difficult. The book, *A Directory of Land Ownership in Scotland c. 1770*, edited by Loretta R. Timperley and published by the Scottish Record Society, is available in many Scottish libraries and archives. It is arranged by county and within county by parish and also gives a list of the landowners in each parish, in most cases (but not always) naming the property which they owned and giving the rateable value, which in turn indicates the size of their holding. There is an index to the names of proprietors – but not of lands. Even if the place in which you are interested is not named, this book provides a guide to the chief landowners of the parish and a search can then be made for muniments for those families (among the Gifts and Deposits in the National Archives of Scotland or other archives) which may be of interest.

The *First (or Old) Statistical Account* (published 1791–99) and *Second (or New) Statistical Account* (published in 1845) often include the names of heritors – or principal landowners – in each parish. For the 17th century and earlier, the printed volumes of the *Register of the Great Seal* (1306–1668) can be very useful as there is an index to places which leads you to a charter and shows who was the owner of the property at the time.

Leases or Tacks

A great many persons who worked the land did not have written leases (referred to as tacks) and for those who did have leases, these have often not survived. Tacks may be found recorded:

- In a register of deeds (in the Burgh Court, Sheriff Court or Books of Council and Session)
- In collections of family papers.

The information given in a tack (also known as an assedation) is usually disappointing from the point of view of the family historian as it will often only state the terms and duration of the contract. Sometimes however there are interesting details of the care the tenant had to take of the property (liming and draining) and occasionally a deed will be found assigning the tack to a son after – or before – his father's death. (See the section on Deeds, page 141.)

Estate Papers

Reference has already been made to the estate papers in the National Archives of Scotland in Gifts and Deposits and to those in local archives or libraries or in private hands. Many collections of family papers still remain with the family concerned. In many cases these have been repertoried in the National Register of Archives. Work is in hand to put the catalogues of the Gifts and Deposits on a computer text base known as 'Clio' which can be searched in the National Archives of Scotland.

Rentals

Some information concerning tenants of all kinds are given in rentals – though again, personal details may be minimal. Most rentals only list the name of the tenant or occupier of the land, the rent paid and sometimes the duration of the tack. On the other hand members of the same family may have occupied a piece of ground over many years and details taken from a continuous series of rentals with 'sightings' of a particular surname may be built up to provide genealogical information about the family.

Estate papers of landowners sometimes include factors' accounts and detailed records of estate management (for example, on the estates of the Dukes of Argyll and Earls of Sutherland) which throw light on people, land use and local conditions. Some of these have been published: check in *Scottish Texts and Calendars* for details of those published by historical clubs or ask in a local library as to what is available.

After the 1745 Jacobite rebellion, a number of estates were forfeited in various parts of Scotland and over the period 1747–76 were administered by the Barons of Exchequer. The Forfeited Estate papers (some of which have been published) are in the National Archives of Scotland among the Exchequer papers – class reference E 700–788. These records contain a great deal of interesting material, including rentals of each estate and reports on conditions there.

Court Papers

If a tenant did not pay his rent, or if the landlord wished to evict him, there may be a record in a court – in the Baron Court, a local court over which the landlord or his factor presided – or in the Sheriff Court. Unless, however, you have knowledge of a particular year or series of years when the tenant might have been in trouble, a long search may be involved in unindexed papers.

Records of the Baron Courts include many names of ordinary people, and provide interesting background information about the management of the estate – regulations about cutting green wood or peats or care of the mill lade, fines for killing game and settlement of local disputes.

The survival of the records of the Baron Courts is fragmentary and it is not always easy to find them. Those in the National Archives of Scotland are listed in *Guide to the National Archives of Scotland* in the section concerning Franchise Courts. Some come under the Gifts and Deposits of the family who were proprietors of the lands concerned: others are in the series known as 'Local Records' class reference RH11. More may be found in local archives and libraries.

Farm Horse Tax

One of the most useful of the series of 18th century taxes was that on farm horses (class reference in the NAS – E326/10). This was levied only in the period 1797–98. The return is arranged by county and by parish within the county and lists all those who had farm horses. It provides an interesting list of farmers of all kinds, land owners and tenants, down to those of modest means. The information given is limited – the name of the farm, the name of the farmer and how many working horses he had – but given the paucity of information about this class of person, the details are welcome.

OCCUPIERS OF LAND

The dividing line between so-called tenants (who perhaps occupied a small acreage of land without a written lease), and crofters and cottars is often vague. Under the terms of the *Royal Commission on the Highlands and Islands* of 1883, a crofter was described as one holding land for agricultural or pastoral purposes directly from a proprietor for an annual rent of not more than £30. A cottar occupied a house at a rent of not more than £2 per annum, but had no land or grazing rights from the proprietor. Terms varied in different parts of the country. Labourers might be paid a daily wage and have no land while others might have a small potato plot or grazing for one beast in return for help on the land.

The *Royal Commission* (also sometimes referred to as the *Napier Commission*) is a valuable source of information about crofters and cottars. Evidence was taken by the parliamentary commissioners at 60 different locations in the Highlands and Islands and much of what was said reflected conditions many years earlier. The actual returns which included the place of residence, names of tenants, numbers of families on the croft and occupations are in the National Archives of Scotland with the records of the Department of Agriculture and Fisheries – class reference AF50.

Genealogical information on cottars and labourers is generally sparse. There may be accounts for a daily wage paid to them in estate accounts but few personal details will be found, apart from those given in parish registers, kirk session records or court records if they offended in some way.

10 THE COURTS

The court system in Scotland is complex, particularly because the administrative functions of various courts overlapped. Thus it may be very difficult to decide in which court a deed is registered, or a case heard concerning debt or crime.

The amount of material making up the records of the various courts, both civil and criminal, is vast and much of it is either difficult to access or of little immediate value to the family historian. There are, however, some classes of records which can reveal a great deal about family history in all its aspects.

Most of the court records are in the National Archives of Scotland, though some of the Franchise or Burgh Court records may be in local archives or with deposits of private papers.

REGISTERS OF DEEDS

Deeds are legal documents, containing in them a clause consenting to registration, concerned with a wide range of matters: business contracts and agreements, marriage settlements, appointment of factors, bonds concerning loans of money and trust dispositions which have already been mentioned in the chapter on testamentary records. Some deeds concern the disposition of land – feu contracts for instance. Not every deed was registered but the consent to have one registered by any competent court meant that it was then legally enforceable. You may also find references to Probative Writs – either in a register of deeds or as a separate register. These were deeds which lacked the registration clause but

THE SCOTTISH COURTS

- The Court of Session – the highest civil court

- The High Court of Justiciary – the highest criminal court

- The Admiralty Court – had jurisdiction in maritime and seafaring cases, both civil and criminal up till 1830

- The Commissary Courts – dealing with executry cases but also dealing with small debt, slander and other civil cases, up to about 1823

- The Sheriff Courts with administrative functions which were both civil and criminal

- The Burgh Courts with local jurisdiction both civil and criminal

- The Justices of the Peace Courts with responsibilities for such matters as general peace keeping, licensing and small debt

- The Franchise Courts which were the local courts of landowners who had been granted particular rights heritably by the Crown to administer justice – both civil and criminal – within their lands. These courts were of **Regality**, **Stewartry** and **Bailiary** (all abolished as heritable jurisdictions in 1748). The fourth Franchise Court, the **Barony Court**, had lesser powers. This was not abolished in 1748 but its remit declined. There are only scattered surviving records for the Franchise Courts. Some are listed in the National Archives of Scotland repertory for RH11: others will be found with the Gifts and Deposits.

concerned matters which required to be recorded. Occasionally a deed was not copied into the register but the original document has survived as a 'Warrant'. In other cases, a whole volume of deeds may have been lost; again, the Warrants may fill the gap. The Warrants (which are bundles of individual papers in boxes) are listed in the repertory of each court.

In many cases, a deed was not registered until long after it was written, which adds to the complications of finding a relevant document. Marriage settlements, for instance, were usually registered at the same time as a trust disposition when one of the parties died – and the winding-up of an estate often involved the production of a number of legal documents.

KINDS OF DEEDS

Any kind of deed may be of value but in cases where there are an enormous number of deeds indexed under the name in which you are interested and a description is given of the type of deed, you should start by considering those labelled marriage contract (shortened as 'mar. cont.'), contract ('cont'), disposition ('disp'), assignation ('assig'), ratification ('ratif'), factory, trust, settlement, or contract of sale. Most bonds and protests are only concerned with a promise – or demand – to repay money and probably contain no genealogical information – though heritable bonds may be of more interest. *The Students' Glossary of Scottish Legal Terms* by Andrew D. Gibb or a legal dictionary such as *A Dictionary & Digest of the Law of Scotland* by George Bell will help you understand the terms used.

Deeds have been described as 'an inexhaustible store of information about the private life of our forefathers' and are an important source for the genealogy and background of people of the past.

There are unfortunately no guidelines as to which register you should search. Your choice will be guided by a consideration of the class of society to which the person belonged and whether indexes exist for the years to be searched. The Books of Council and Session tend to be used by the better-off members of society such as landowners, particularly from the 18th century onwards, while tenant farmers, craftsmen and lesser merchants often used the Sheriff Court or the burgh court. The Commissary Court (only up to c. 1823) contains settlements and legal matters of all members of society. There are only fragments of registers of deeds in the Franchise Courts and these should be the source of last recourse. In general, it is advisable first to search the registers which have easiest access through indexes.

The Books of Council & Session

This is a vast series of registers of deeds kept in the National Archives of Scotland (class reference RD) and unless you are interested in a period covered by indexes, it is better to avoid the task. There are three series of registers of deeds:

- First Series (RD1) 1554–1649 and 1652–57. There is a calendar of deeds for the years 1554–95 with indexes to persons 1554–90. There are earlier deeds in Court of Session books from 1501–81 (with a few gaps) – class reference CS5-6 in part covered by calendars and indexes. There is no indexing from 1596–1660 and searching has to be done with the aid of minute books; but as there were several clerks recording deeds concurrently in his own register, the task is enormous unless you have an exact date of registration.

- Second Series (RD2-4) 1661–1811. There are annual indexes to the registers for the years 1661–1702, 1705–07, 1714–15, 1750–52 and 1770–1811. As in the previous period, the registers are compiled in several offices, Dalrymple, Durie and Mackenzie and a deed might be recorded in any one of these registers. It is essential when searching these indexes to note the office in which the deed was recorded, shortened as 'Dal', 'Dur' or 'Mack'. To order up a deed, put 'RD' on the slip, followed by the number given to the particular office (Dal = 2; Dur = 3; Mack = 4) followed by the volume number given in the index. The last number in the index is a folio number which does not need to be put on the order form.

- Third Series (RD5) 1812 to the present. There are annual indexes to the whole series. The indexes up to 1850 are in the Historical Search Room but the later ones can be consulted downstairs in the National Archives of Scotland Legal Search Room. To order up a deed from this series, put 'RD5' on your slip, plus the number of the volume given in the index. Even if the indexes are downstairs, all documents should be ordered upstairs, in the Historical Reading Room.

The earlier indexes refer to all the principal parties concerned. From 1661 to 1683, the index shows the type of deed registered (contract, bond, disposition, etc.) but this information is omitted in the rest of the second series indexes. From 1770 onwards, only the name of the granter is indexed, the name of the grantee and nature of the deed being given alongside.

Sheriff Court Registers of Deeds

The boundaries of the sheriffdoms varied from time to time but in general they were similar to the old county boundaries. In some counties, however, there was more than one Sheriff Court: in Angus, Argyll, Ayr, Edinburgh, Fife, Inverness, Lanark, Perth, Renfrew, Ross & Cromarty, Stirling and Wigtown. In most cases, only one of the courts in each county kept a register of deeds. The Sheriff Court registers of deeds (with the exception of those for Orkney and Shetland which are held in the respective archives) are in the National Archives of Scotland.

Lacking indexes, there may be minute books which refer to the deeds in chronological order, and provide a varying amount of information about the content, the type of document (bond, disposition, factory, etc.) and the chief parties concerned. Gaps in the registers may sometimes be filled by warrants.

INDEXES TO SHERIFF COURT REGISTERS OF DEEDS

There is little indexing of registers of deeds in the Sheriff Courts before the 19th century and not all are indexed after that time. The following is a list of those for which there are indexes:

Ayr (SC6)	1800–99
Cromarty (SC24)	1819–1900
Cupar, Fife (SC20)	1719–99; 1809–1900
Dingwall, Ross & Cromarty (SC25)	1794–1889
Dunblane, Perthshire (SC44)	1809–1902
Dunoon, Argyllshire (SC51)	1809–88
Haddington, East Lothian (SC40)	1809–94
Hamilton, Lanarkshire (SC37)	1810–97
Kirkcudbright (SC16)	1623–1700 (published: copy in NAS Library)
Linlithgow, West Lothian (SC41)	1809–94
Paisley, Renfrewshire (SC58)	1809–99
Perth (SC49)	1809–1901
Stirling (SC67)	1809–1900
Tain, Ross & Cromarty (SC34)	1812–84

Burgh Registers of Deeds

Few burgh registers of deeds are indexed but as they are more local in coverage and less bulky in content, it is not too difficult or time-consuming to go through the registers looking for something of interest. In many volumes there are side-heads naming the granter and nature of the deed which make searching easier. Consult the repertory of the particular burgh to find out what is available.

Commissary Court Registers of Deeds

Constituted as a civil court after the Reformation, it was competent to register deeds of all kinds though, in keeping with its particular remit in dealing with marriage, inheritance and executry, you may find a number of dispositions and marriage settlements. The Commissary Court registers of deeds are usually covered by the manuscript lists of contents for each Commissary Court. Consult the repertory of the Commissary Court covering the area in which you are interested and on the first page check whether there is a reference to an 'Inventory of Records'. This should include a 'List of Deeds'. These deeds will not be copied into a volume and will be produced as a bundle of documents covering the year of registration of the deed.

Franchise Court Registers of Deeds

Only the courts of Regality, Stewartry and Bailiary had the right to register deeds. Few have survived but check the RH11 repertory.

Notarial Records – Protocol Books

The books of the notaries public contained formal evidence of
transactions between various parties and are a valuable source of
information about legal dealings – settlements, tacks, loans and
many other matters (including sasines which have been mentioned earlier) – particularly for the 16th and early 17th centuries.
Many were written in Latin and unless they have been published
and indexed they are a difficult source to use. A list of those in
the National Archives of Scotland (class reference NP) is given in
Guide to the National Archives of Scotland and indicates the area
covered by the particular protocol book as well as the starting
date. The NP repertory in the National Archives of Scotland indicates whether the book has been published. Royal burghs also had
the right to keep protocol books. Consult the relevant burgh repertory in the National Archives of Scotland or in the local archive.

DEBT

An enormous number of people of all classes were taken to court
for debt but because of the difficulty of determining in which
court a case was heard, a search may require a considerable degree
of dedication and if found, may contain little of value. Debt cases
are recorded in the records of the Justices of the Peace (class reference JP in the National Archives of Scotland), in the Burgh
Court, Sheriff Court or Court of Session, in the Commissary
Courts and in the diligence records (National Archives of
Scotland class reference DI.) Those heard in the JP, Commissary
and Burgh Courts were usually for small sums of money and the

evidence heard may provide interesting vignettes of local life. Debt cases sometimes include genealogical information, for example, when the debtor dies and his family are burdened with the debt.

Diligence Records

Diligence was a procedure used against a debtor by a decree of court. Under a *horning* he was ordered to discharge his debt within a given time and if he failed to comply, his moveable goods might be poinded. Letters of *inhibition* prevented the debtor from selling or burdening his heritable estate before the debt was paid, while under an *apprising* (or *adjudication*) an order could be made to sell the heritable property of the debtor. There are General Registers of Hornings, Inhibitions and Apprisings dating back to the first half of the 17th century concerned with cases over the whole of Scotland and Particular Registers of Hornings and Inhibitions for the sheriffdoms. Bailiaries, Stewartries and Regalities also kept registers of this nature. There is a useful list of all these registers in *Guide to the National Archives of Scotland*. From 1781 onwards there are a number of printed indexes to these registers which can be consulted in the National Archives of Scotland. Lacking indexes, minute books (which often give quite detailed information) have to be used.

Bankruptcy

References in the indexes to Inhibitions and Apprisings may indicate that a sequestration was involved and that the person had gone bankrupt. This will lead you to a case heard in the Court of Session. The records are held by the National Archives of

Scotland in West Register House. There is a useful guide to the complicated procedure to locate the documentation of such cases in *Tracing Your Scottish Ancestors* by Cecil Sinclair.

Some such cases involved the production of business books, personal or family papers as evidence which are a treasure-trove of fascinating detail about the past. The List and Index Society has published a *List of Court of Session Productions*, indexing all these productions under the name of the person concerned, by place and by type of business for the period c. 1760–1840. There is also a microfiche index to later productions. Although a large proportion of the cases are concerned with the claims of creditors, some productions are from other cases heard before the Court of Session and, as well as financial evidence, you will find rentals, inventories of all kinds and evidence of family births and marriages. The productions can be ordered up at West Register House.

Processes

In the repertories of the various courts, there is usually a section titled 'Processes'. These are all the papers and evidence presented in the course of an action. If you know the approximate date of a case and the court in which it was heard, much information can be gained from this material, but because of its bulk, it is not possible to 'browse' effectively. There are some indexes to the processes of the Court of Session and details of these will be found in *Guide to the National Archives of Scotland*. For other courts, diet, roll and minute books provide searching aids to details of the various cases, both civil and criminal. In some of the Commissary Courts, there are inventories of processes.

CRIMINAL CASES

The initial problem is to determine in which court a case may have been heard and to what higher court it may have been referred. The Barony Courts, other Franchise Courts (up to 1747), JP and Burgh Courts were mainly concerned with the keeping of 'good neighbourhood', theft, breach of the peace and breaking of game or licensing law, though before the 18th century these courts, with the exception of the JP Court, had the power to administer a death sentence in certain cases. In these courts, criminal and civil cases were often intermingled.

For those who committed serious crimes between 1812 and 1900, there is an easily accessible index to Precognitions – written reports of the evidence given by witnesses. The Precognitions are kept with the records of the Lord Advocate (NAS class reference AD). There is a card catalogue in West Register House, arranged alphabetically under the name of the accused with a brief statement of the crime. This index is particularly useful in locating cases for which the sentence was transportation. Precognitions may contain a great deal of family history and background, though sometimes it seems the evidence given was not always the truth.

Books of Adjournal and minute books for the High Court of Justiciary and for the Court when it was on circuit (NAS class reference JC) give details of the various trials. Search the repertory for minute books, roll books or books of adjournal, which can be used as searching aids.

Some court records – particularly early ones – have been printed. Most of these will be listed in *Scottish Texts and Calendars*.

11 TAXATION & TRADE

Records of trade and taxation often appear as poor diet for the family historian but this material should not be overlooked and may sometimes be a source of vital clues in tracing ancestors. In the case of trade records, these may fill out the background to the family as well as giving nominal information and sometimes valuable genealogical information about those involved in business.

TAXATION

Two taxes were levied by the Government in Scotland in the 1690s. Neither are complete for the whole country and the Poll Tax provides far more personal details than the earlier Hearth Tax.

Hearth Tax

This tax, due on every hearth in Scotland, and payable by both landowners and tenants, was levied between 1691 and 1695. Not all the returns have survived and many returns are deficient. Of schedules that are extant, some relate to the owners of the hearths, not mentioning the rest of the household, and others only refer to the accounts of money collected without giving any names. Another drawback to these records is that a landowner might collect the tax for those liable for Hearth Tax on his estate and individuals are not listed.

To find out what has survived, consult the repertory for Exchequer Records (NAS reference E69). This details the extant records for each county, the returns will be arranged by parish within the county. Some of the tax returns are with family papers – there will be a reference to these in the E69 repertory.

The volume, *West Lothian Hearth Tax 1691*, edited by Duncan Adamson, gives a complete transcript of the tax returns for the county and also an abstract of the returns for the rest of Scotland, showing the nature of surviving records for each parish, and where they are to be found.

Copies of some of the Hearth Tax returns are in LDS Libraries. Abstracts and indexes to the Hearth Tax returns for Stirlingshire and Perthshire are published in the volumes of *Monumental Inscriptions* for these counties compiled by J.F. Mitchell. These lists are useful in providing evidence as to whether families of a certain surname were resident in a particular parish at the end of the 17th century.

Poll Tax

The Poll Tax, paid by all adults (persons of 16 or over) including the children of the rich but excepting the poor, was collected between 1693 and 1699. Again, the coverage for the country is not complete. Check the NAS repertory E70. There is a list for each county and also notes of surviving returns recorded else-where. Some have been published – including those for Aberdeenshire (published by the Spalding Club) – and these are noted in the E70 repertory.

As with the Hearth Tax, not all the Poll Tax returns have survived and the information given in the lists varies greatly. In Aberdeenshire, for example, an entry will name the persons in the household (mentioning though not always naming the wife and children) including the servants, giving the occupations of each. Other returns name all persons, including wives and children but some include few names, are very imperfect or lacking altogether.

Taxation in the Royal Burghs

Money was raised for various causes in the royal burghs through stent or cess rolls (levied on land). If your ancestor lived in a royal burgh, his name may appear in one of these returns. Consult the repertory of the records of the particular burgh (either in the National Archives of Scotland or in a local archive) to see if there is a relevant reference. The Scottish Records Association *Datasheets* with summaries of archival holdings may also mention them.

18th-Century Taxes

From 1748 onwards, taxes were levied on various commodities, sometimes just for one year, sometimes over a series of years. The class reference in the National Archives of Scotland is E326. These taxes were charged on windows (1748–98), inhabited houses (1778–98), retail shops (1785–89), male and female servants (1777–98 and 1785–92 respectively), dogs, clocks, watches, carts, carriages and farm horses (see page 139) for short periods. A great many people avoided or were not liable to pay tax and therefore the number of persons listed in the tax returns is relatively small. For example, a house had to have at least seven windows or an annual rent of £5 to become liable for the tax and thus most were exempted. With the exception of the Farm Horse Tax, unless the family was relatively well-to-do, these records will be of little value.

TRADE

Quarterly Customs Accounts

Scottish trade – both overseas and coastal – was closely supervised. The Customs Collectors were responsible for keeping quarterly returns of all ships entering or leaving the ports in their precincts carrying cargoes liable for duty. Quarterly Customs Accounts (NAS class reference E504) are arranged by port and give the date, name the ship, her port of registration, the port from which she had sailed, or for which she was bound, give a description of her cargo, the name of her master and the name of the local merchant (often one of the owners) who was responsible for the cargo.

Although each record includes limited information about individuals, a study of these registers can result in an interesting picture of the career of a particular master of a ship, or the involvement of local merchants in trade.

Most of the Quarterly Customs Accounts cover the period 1742–1830, though for some ports, the returns commence later. There is a gap in the records for all ports from 1796–1805 and 1807–10.

Ports for which there are records are: Alloa, Anstruther, Ayr, Banff, Bo'ness, Campbeltown, Dumfries, Dunbar, Dundee, Fort William, Glasgow, Grangemouth, Inverkeithing, Inverness, Irvine, Isle Martin, Kirkcaldy, Kirkcudbright, Leith, Lochbroom, Montrose, Oban, Orkney, Perth, Port Glasgow, Port Patrick, Prestonpans, Rothesay, Shetland, Stornoway, Stranraer, Thurso, Tobermory, Wick and Wigtown.

Bounties on Whaling and Buss Herring Fishing

From 1750 to 1825, the Government encouraged whaling by offering bounties. In order to claim the money, the masters had to keep records (NAS E508) which provide details of the ship's name, the port to which she belonged, her tonnage, her catch and – of more interest – the name of her master, mate, surgeon and crew (harpooners, steersmen, line-managers, sailors and apprentices).

The bounties given for fitting out decked ships of between 20 and 80 tons, known as busses, for the herring fishing over the years 1752–96 were also dependent on fulfilling strict regulations and the return of detailed papers (Customs Cash Vouchers – also E508). These buss papers name the ship, the port to which she belonged, her catch and the names of all her crew and from 1770 onwards include information on age, height, colour of hair and place of birth (usually the parish, but sometimes the township, or just the county or island). The number of busses sailing each year varied greatly but rose to several hundred in the third quarter of the century. Unfortunately, although the Cash Accounts (E502) act as a searching aid in naming the ship, the port to which she belonged and the year when she received the bounty, they do not help in locating an individual who might have signed on any ship for the three-month fishing season. Work is in progress in indexing buss crew lists.

Customs Letter Books

For most ports, correspondence has survived between the local Collector of Customs at each port and the Board in Edinburgh (there are also instructions issued by the Board to the local collectors but these are of less value to the family historian). The letter books of a number of ports start in the early decades of the 18th century and some continue into the 19th century. The Outport Records (as they are officially known) form part of the records of Customs and Excise. Some of these records are in the NAS (class reference CE) but others are in local archives; Glasgow Archives hold most of those for West Coast ports.

The letter books include much interesting material concerning local trading conditions and provide a detailed picture of the smuggling trade. They also give personal details of the customs staff – lists of officers serving at each port, appointments and deaths. Further information on those serving on the Scottish Board of Customs between 1707 and 1829 is given in the establishment books of the Scottish Board (CE3 and CE12) and in the salary books (E502). There are two mid-18th century lists of customs officers in the NAS: GD1/372/1 dated 1752 and RH2/8/102 dated 1755. Both give notes on the character of the officers and the 1752 list also gives birthplace and marital status.

A list of excise officers serving between 1707 and 1830 has been compiled by J.F. Mitchell and can be consulted in NAS on microfilm (RH4/6/1–2). Further information on customs and excise records is given in Cecil Sinclair's two books, *Tracing Scottish Local History* and *Tracing Your Scottish Ancestors*.

Business Records

Records of businesses, factories, shops and other enterprises can throw light on entrepreneurs and owners, the workforce and their backgrounds. Some of these records are in the National Archives of Scotland – check the Summary Catalogue under the name of the business. The National Archives of Scotland also hold the records of the National Coal Board, Gas Board, North of Scotland Hydro-Electric Board, South of Scotland Electricity Board and British Steel and of the railway companies operating in Scotland (class reference for the railways BR). Check the NRA(S) Index which has references to business archives over the whole of Scotland under either the name of the firm or under a category, for example, banks, building trades, etc.

The Business Record Centre (part of the University of Glasgow Archives) at 13 Thurso Street, Glasgow, holds the largest dedicated collection of business records in Europe, a number of them going back to the 18th century.

References to primary sources for businesses and industries will be found in bibliographies and notes in books written about particular firms or industries. *Studies in Scottish Business History*, edited by Peter Payne, contains a great deal of useful information on printed works and archival material on Scottish enterprise, both in Scotland and in America and Australia.

Many firms got into financial difficulties and were involved in Court of Session cases. The productions – that is, business books or papers produced as evidence – are often extremely informative. Consult *Scottish Record Office Court of Session Productions c.1760–1840*. The productions can be consulted at West Register House in Edinburgh.

The amount of information given about individuals varies enormously in business papers. If your ancestors were in business, then you may find a great deal of detail about their financial dealings. A worker in a factory is more difficult to document but there may be records of pay or contributions to a welfare fund.

A Catalogue of some Labour Records in Scotland, compiled by Ian MacDougall, gives details of records of trade unions, friendly societies, Scottish local societies and political parties, some of which include lists of members and returns of sickness and mortality. Most of the records are for the 19th century, but some go back further.

PARLIAMENTARY REPORTS AND PAPERS

From the 18th century onwards, Parliamentary Commissions have produced reports on a wide variety of subjects, for example, agriculture, emigration, education, the poor, and on all aspects of industry such as employment of women and children, wages, the fisheries, mining and weaving. The information in these reports has been referred to as 'buried treasure'. They are an invaluable source of information as to how our ancestors lived, dealing with working conditions, housing and many other aspects of life and death, but they also include names as evidence was gathered from many persons. *Scotland in the 19th century – An Analytical Biography of Material Relating to Scotland in Parliamentary Papers 1800–1900*, compiled by JA Haythornthwaite, is a guide to what is covered by these papers. *Lists of Parliamentary Papers 1696–1965* (three volumes), edited by P & G Ford, should also be consulted. This covers English as well as Scottish material.

Merchants & Traders in the Royal Burghs

When a royal burgh was given its charter, one of the most important privileges granted was that of the right of the burgesses to be involved in trade – particularly overseas. To find out when and if a town was erected into a royal burgh, consult *The Burghs of Scotland – A Critical List*, by George Smith Pryde.

Records of the admission of burgesses have not all survived though a number are extant and some have been printed, including those for Aberdeen, Canongate, Dumbarton, Dumfries, Edinburgh, Glasgow, Stirling, Inveraray and Banff. Check with the local family history society, library or archive in the area in which you are interested. Records of admission will often be found in the town council minutes or burgh accounts.

Burgess records may be very useful, particularly if someone was admitted as son of a burgess. Sometimes it is possible to trace a family back several generations through the burgess admissions alone. If a man was admitted through marrying the daughter of a burgess, this can lead to a marriage entry, but indicates that either his family did not have burgess status or had come to the burgh from elsewhere. This can also be deduced from cases where burgess status is purchased.

Burgess Guilds & Incorporations

The burgesses in most burghs formed themselves into guilds – the merchant guilds and the craft guilds. Members of the merchant guilds dominated the town councils and lists of council members annually in the town council minutes of each burgh. These council minutes are a valuable source of local social history and include the names of many persons living in the burgh.

The craft guilds – for such occupations as wrights, hammermen, tailors, weavers, bakers, coopers and cordiners – aimed to see that competition was not offered by 'unfreemen' and to regulate the standard of craft work. One of their duties was to oversee the apprentice craftsmen and test their 'assays' – pieces of work which would be the final test before they were admitted as guild brothers. The guilds also cared for the widows and children of members. The records of merchant and craft guilds sometimes contain lists of members, details of apprenticeships and of pastoral care of members' families.

Overall, few apprenticeship records have survived. There may be an apprenticeship agreement in any register of deeds, often naming the father of the apprentice. Unless the register of deeds is indexed, such documents may be hard to locate. Some burghs do have registers of apprentices – Inverness, for example, has a register of apprentice indentures covering the period 1738–1846. The apprentice records for Edinburgh have been printed by the Scottish Record Society for the years 1583–1800 and name the person to whom each was apprenticed with the date of admission. Most apprentices were in their early- or mid-teens when admitted. Following the levy of stamp duty on indentures of apprentices in 1710 (made in London) a list was kept of apprentices covering the years 1710–1811 and has been indexed. This is in the Public Record Office in London and includes some – but not all – Scottish apprentices. It can also be consulted at the Society of Genealogists in London.

MEANS OF BECOMING A BURGESS

Most burgesses were men but occasionally a woman was admitted. A person might become a burgess in various ways:

- As the son of a burgess
- By marrying the daughter of a burgess
- By serving an apprenticeship
- By purchase
- By being created an honorary burgess or as a reward for a service.

Extant records vary from burgh to burgh and may take a little time to track down. Check the repertories of the individual burghs (NAS class reference B) to find what is listed for each burgh. Some of the guildry records are in the Gifts and Deposits or in the Exchequer records, so also check the NAS *Summary Catalogue* under the name of the burgh. For example, the *Summary Catalogue* shows that Ayr burgh records are referenced B6 but there is another entry under 'Ayr – Weavers' Incorporation' showing that these records are with the Exchequer Records under E870.

Some references to guild records are given in the NRA(S) Index. Look under the name of the burgh or in the classified index under Guilds and Incorporations.

Many of the burgh records held in the local archives include those of the guilds. Stirling, for example, has records for the incorporations of bakers, cordiners, fleshers, hammermen, skinners, tailors, weavers and mechanics, some going back to the 15th century.

12 MAPS & PLANS

Maps and plans are of importance and interest to family historians in a number of ways:

- In identifying places where people lived
- In building up a knowledge of a particular place or district
- In noting boundaries of parishes, sheriffdoms or counties which may be important in locating relevant records
- In giving details of names of proprietors and sometimes of tenants: these details are only found on some maps and plans.

The National Library Map Library at Causewayside Building, Edinburgh has a vast collection of maps of Scotland and elsewhere – mainly printed ones. It is open Monday to Friday and until midday on Saturday. There is a photocopying service.

The NAS at West Register House hold a very large collection of manuscript maps and plans emanating from government departments, the nationalised industries including the railways, court actions, and private papers. *Descriptive Lists of Plans in the Scottish Record Office vols. 1–4* have been published by HMSO and give details (arranged by county and by parish within the county) of many of the plans held by the NAS. There is a card index of all maps and plans held in West Register House arranged on a topographical basis.

The University of Glasgow Business Record Centre holds an important collection of plans and photographs relating to many industries including shipbuilders, distillers and railways.

The National Monuments Record of Scotland, 16 Bernard Street, Edinburgh holds collections of architectural records of buildings in the form of plans, drawings and photographs.

Local archives and district offices also hold collections of maps and plans of local interest of both private and public provenance.

ORDNANCE SURVEY MAPS

In 1855 – after much argument – a national survey was authorised on the scale 1:2500 (25 inches to the mile) for the most populous parts of Scotland and in the following three decades the whole country was mapped on the scale of 6 inches to the mile. In connection with the 6-inch and 25-inch scale maps, the surveyors compiled name books of all places appearing on these maps. The name books are arranged by county and by parish within each county. Information given for each place name includes spelling variants, situation of the place and descriptions of villages, hills, rivers, streets, bridges, buildings and forests. The name books can be consulted on microfilm at the National Archives of Scotland – reference RH4/23.

In connection with the 25-inch maps, there are also *Books of Reference* which give details of acreage and lands use linked to references on the map. These cover much of central Scotland, the Borders, and lowland areas of Grampian and Perthshire. Fife, Midlothian, East Lothian, Wigtownshire and Kirkcudbrightshire are not covered.

The first edition of the one-inch ordnance survey maps of Scotland was the result of a survey carried out in 1864–5, first published in 1872 and revised in 1895. The revised edition has

---

DETAILS ON MAPS

Information on maps – places named or omitted, emphasis on settlements, roads and geographical features – depends on the reason for producing the map but also sometimes on the whim of the surveyor or cartographer. Some place-names may only be included not because of their importance but because they fitted the available space on the map. Spelling of place-names is often phonetic rather than accurate. It is important to assess the information given on maps and to try to interpret what is presented.

---

been reprinted by Caledonian Books, Collieston, Ellon, Aberdeenshire AB41 8RT, Scotland (116 sheets cover the whole country) and can be purchased. Many libraries and archives have copies of these maps. Later editions of the ordnance survey maps provide interesting comparisons with earlier ones.

PRE-1850 MAPS OF SCOTLAND

A comprehensive guide to maps of Scotland from the 16th century onwards, showing the scale and where copies can be consulted is provided by *The Early Maps of Scotland,* published by the Royal Scottish Geographical Society. Volume 1 deals with maps of the whole of Scotland; Volume 2 covers county maps, town plans and specialised maps and plans.

COUNTY MAPS

To find out what is available for each county, consult Volume 2 of

Early Maps of Scotland. The earliest atlas is that of Joannis Blaeu, published in 1654 and reprinted in 1991 by Studio Editions Ltd. There are many later individual county maps drawn to various scales; some of the most useful are those produced by John Thomson between 1805 and 1830.

TOWN PLANS

The earliest surviving plan of a Scottish town is one of Edinburgh in 1544, but most town plans date to the 19th century. In 1828 John Wood published a volume of 48 Scottish town plans and there are another five which were not included in his *Atlas*. These maps provide a great deal of detail, showing houses, gardens, street layout and include the names of proprietors of the various properties at the time. They have been reprinted and can be purchased or consulted at various libraries and archives.

The *Boundaries Report* of 1832 also resulted in a number of large-scale town plans and 75 plans were produced on the scale of 6 inches to the mile.

PLANS

Legal disputes over boundaries, mapping of estates by landowners, the planning of new towns, building of canals, roads and railways and division of commonties have all resulted in a the production of plans. These can provide a great deal of detail and estate plans may include names of proprietors, sometimes name tenants or occupiers and show land usage. Some plans are beautifully illustrated.

Work is in progress on the NAS collection to allow access to the collection through a database which can be searched by place, subject, or surveyor. There will be terminals in the search rooms of both the West and Historical Search Rooms. Many of the plans are outhoused and 48 hours' notice of consultation is required.

13 PEOPLE & PROFESSIONS

Various records have been covered which provide information on many classes of person, but the following sections will serve as an additional guide to particular records to document the lives and careers of certain people and professions. *Scottish Trades and Professions – a Selected Bibliography*, compiled by D.R. Torrance, lists books in connection with a wide range of occupations; bibliographies given in those volumes will lead to wider study on a particular topic.

THE ARMY & MILITIA

The British Army

From the time of the Union of England and Scotland, the Army was the British Army and therefore most records are in the Public Record Office at Kew, London. *Army Records for Family Historians*, by Simon Fowler, is an excellent guide to what is available and how to find it. *My Ancestor Was in the British Army*, by M.J. Watts and Christopher T. Watts, and *Army Service Records of the First World War*, by S. Fowler, W. Spencer and S. Tamblin, are also useful.

Other records are in local repositories throughout Britain and in regimental museums. Norman Holding has compiled a list of records for the First World War and where they may be found in *The Location of British Army Records – a National Directory of World War I Sources*. The National Army Museum (Royal Hospital Road, London SW3 4HT) holds a large collection of private and regimental papers relating to the British Army, the Indian Army (prior to 1947) and British Colonial Forces. For particular regiments, it is worth contacting the regimental museum. *A Guide to Military Museums* by Terence Wise lists these with their addresses.

Records in the National Archives of Scotland relating to regiments and campaigns are catalogued in *A Military Source List – A Guide to Military Records in the Scottish Record Office (Parts 1 and 2)*. Part 1 is a guide to sources on military records in private archives held in NAS and Part 2 deals with sources on military history in government and other records held in the same archive. Part 1 is indexed by regiment or unit, and by battle or campaign; Part 2 is unindexed. The scope of the papers catalogued is wide and deals with military matters in Scotland at all periods – for example, a list of nobles and lairds to supply a thousand men with spears for an expedition to the Isles in 1591, or lists of prisoners with Heyder Ally in India in 1780.

The East India Company

The East India Company was founded in 1601 as a trading company but became a vast administrative organisation in which many Scots served as merchants and civil servants, or as soldiers or sailors. The records are housed at the India Office Library, 197 Blackfriars Road, London SE1 8NG, and include a great deal of genealogical information about those who served in the company.

The Militia, Fencibles & Volunteers

Militia, fencible and volunteer forces have been raised in Scotland for home defence – usually on a short-term service basis – since the 17th century and played a particularly prominent role at the time of the Napoleonic Wars at the end of the 18th century and early years of the 19th century. Fencible regiments were composed of men who had enlisted voluntarily to serve in England, Scotland or Ireland and were usually raised by the landowners. The volunteers were local bodies of men acting in the capacity of a 'home guard' at the time of the Napoleonic War. The militia was instituted under the Militia Act (Scotland) of 1797 and provided for a national force. Men were balloted from those listed in each parish between certain age limits and served a term of compulsory service – though it was possible for a balloted man to pay for a substitute to serve in his place. Some persons were exempt – such as those with more than two children under the age of ten,

INFORMATION IN MILITIA RECORDS

When studying militia records it is important to note whether the names are of all those liable for military service between certain ages (lists often taken by the parish schoolmaster of those usually between 18 and 45) or whether they are the lists of those actually selected by ballot to serve in the militia according to the quota laid down for the parish.

The information given in the lists of those liable for service or balloted varies. They may include details of place of residence, occupation, and give age, parish of birth and sometimes a personal description. Oaths taken on enlistment, regimental returns and applications for dependants' allowances may also fill out the information given about individuals.

and those in certain occupations such as schoolmasters, ministers and apprentices. The responsibility of organising the raising of the militia belonged to the Lord Lieutenant in each county.

Many records relating to the raising and organising of the fencible, volunteer and militia forces are in the muniments of the local landowners. Consult Volume 1 of *A Military Source List* for those held in NAS, but other records will be found among family papers held in other archives throughout Scotland. NRA(S) lists should also be checked for records still in private hands.

Some militia records are with the Sheriff Courts (see Volume 2 of the *Military Source List*). Burgh Court records also include a few. The Lieutenancy records which contain a number of listings in connection with the militia are mostly in district archives or in local libraries. A useful list has been compiled by Professor Arnold Morrison – *Some Scottish Sources on Militias, Fencibles and Volunteers* – and can be obtained from him at 4 Victoria Place, Stirling FK8 2QX.

The Public Record Office in London also holds some records. *Militia Lists and Musters 1757–1876*, by Jeremy Gibson and Mervyn Medlycott, has a section on Scottish militia.

THE CHURCH

The Church of Scotland

Biographical details of all ministers of the Church of Scotland from the Reformation (1560) are given in *Fasti Ecclesiae Scoticanae*, edited by Hew Scott. The volumes are arranged by synods and by parishes within the synods. There is a volume of corrections and additions and final volumes cover the period 1929–75. Information given covers the career of each minister as well as details of his family and published works. It is a valuable work of reference though there are some errors and omissions.

The period from the Reformation to 1638 is also covered by *Fasti Ecclesiae Scoticanae Medii Aevi ad annum 1638*, by D.E.R. Watt but it provides few personal details.

Records of the Presbyteries and Synods contain a certain amount of information about ministers (NAS – reference CH2) but, being unindexed, they are time-consuming to search unless the date of a particular matter is known. Church of Scotland General Assembly Papers (CH1) are catalogued chronologically and some cases concern ministers.

Dissenting Churches

Several books give details of non-Church of Scotland ministers:

- *The Reformed Presbyterian Church in Scotland, its Congregations, Ministers and Students 1743–1876*, by W.J. Couper
- *Annals and Statistics of the United Presbyterian Church*, by W. MacKelvie
- *History of the Congregations of the United Presbyterian Church from 1733–1900*, by R. Small
- *Annals of the Free Church of Scotland 1843–1900*, by W. Ewing
- *Fasti of the United Free Church of Scotland 1900–1929*, by J.A. Lamb

• The New College Library at the Mound, Edinburgh EH1 2LU, holds a considerable amount of material on the Free Church, United Presbyterian congregations and on the Church of Scotland, including portraits of leading Scottish churchmen.

The Episcopal Church

An index to the clergymen of the Episcopal Church in Scotland as listed in the *Year Books* of the church for the 18th centuries onwards up to 1955 has been compiled by E.W. Binning and can be consulted in New Register House.

Roman Catholic Clergy

The names of Roman Catholic secular clergy for the years 1732–1878 are given in *The Innes Review* (Scottish Catholic Historical Association), Vols. 17, 34 and 40. The Scottish Catholic Archives at Columba House, 16 Drummond Place, Edinburgh EH3 6PL (open by appointment) have considerable holdings (summarised in the *Scottish Records Association Datasheet No.6*).

Fasti Ecclesiae Scoticanae Medii Aevi ad annum 1638, by D.E.R. Watt, spans the pre- and post-Reformation (1560) period but it provides few personal details.

GENTRY

Earlier chapters have dealt with many of the records which will document the lives and families of landowners such as deeds, sasines and family muniments. A great deal has been written about the landed gentry and the peerage but printed works should be viewed with some reserve as many contain a considerable number of errors.

There are two books of value in finding out what has been published on a particular family or person and it is wise to consult both: *Scottish Family Histories*, by Joan P.S. Ferguson, and *Scottish Family History*, by Margaret Stuart. Joan Ferguson's book also notes where copies of a book can be consulted.

Burke's Peerage and *Burke's Landed Gentry* (various editions) cover an enormous number of families. A contribution concerning a family may be printed in one edition but omitted from another. There is a separate volume which is an index showing in which volume or volumes an entry for a particular family occurs in the *Peerage* and *Landed Gentry*. Entries have been submitted by the family concerned and there are in some cases omissions or errors. *The Scots Peerage* (nine volumes) by Sir James Balfour Paul contains a great deal of information. The copy on the shelves in NAS is annotated with corrections and additions which have been made by staff.

The Dictionary of National Biography gives details of famous persons of all classes of society. The information given is not always accurate or complete.

Manuscript genealogies of many families will be found in NAS among the papers of individual families and there is also a collection of genealogies (indexed) in RH16. Check the National Library, the library of the Scottish Genealogy Society, other local archives and NRA(S) to see what is in private hands. As with printed works, do not always accept what is recorded in manuscript genealogies as correct.

Court of the Lord Lyon

The Lord Lyon King of Arms controls armorial matters and the matriculation of arms. The Lyon Office is in New Register House, Edinburgh and the records include the *Public Register of All Arms and Bearings in Scotland*, which commenced in 1672. The Lyon Office is also the repository of a number of recorded genealogies, as well as of a private collection of families' histories and genealogies – both printed and in manuscript. The nine volumes of *Birth Briefs, Funeral Entries and Funeral Escutcheons* have been printed and published by the Scottish Record Society. If you wish to consult the records at the Lyon Office, you should write to the Court of the Lord Lyon, HM New Register House, Edinburgh EH1 3YT or telephone first – 0131 556 7255. There is a fee for having searches made in the records there.

LAWYERS

The two main classes of lawyers are advocates, who could plead in the Court of Session and solicitors, known in Scotland as 'writers' – some of whom are Writers to the Signet. Judges are usually appointed from among the advocates. Judges appointed up to 1832 are listed in *Senators of the Court of Justice*, by Brunton and Haig. *The Lord Advocates of Scotland*, by G.W.T. Ormond, is pub-

> It is also worth bearing in mind that sometimes later generations 'upgraded' the occupations of their ancestors and someone termed a Writer to the Signet may in fact have been just a writer.

lished in three volumes. Details of advocates (including brief biographical notes) are given in *The Faculty of Advocates 1532–1943* and of Writers to the Signet (usually shortened to WS) in *History of the Society of Writers to Her Majesty's Signet*, which includes some personal details of members from 1594 to 1890. These books, which should be available in many libraries, are useful but do not name everyone, especially in early years. Lawyers who pleaded causes in the Sheriff Courts or lower courts were known as procurators and in Aberdeen (only) procurators were known as advocates. The New Spalding Club in 1912 published a *History of the Society of Advocates in Aberdeen.*

Writers who were authorised to certify legal documents were admitted as notaries. Records of the admission of notaries are held in the National Archives of Scotland – class reference NP2. The Register of Admission of Notaries goes back to 1563 but has some deficiencies which may be filled by the warrants of admission. Some of the entries give place of birth, age and name of the writer's father.

THE POOR

Up until the passing of the Poor Law Act of 1845, the kirk sessions were responsible for the care of the poor. Under the Act, parochial boards were established to deal with poor relief in each parish. These may be listed with the heritors' records in the NAS and some will be found in the CO catalogue there under the relevant county. Most of the parochial board records are in the district archives or with council records kept locally. Some of the returns of aid given to the poor are very detailed with information on family circumstances, ages and place of birth. Glasgow poor relief applications for the second half of the 19th century have been put on a database which can be searched at the Glasgow City Archives.

THE MEDICAL PROFESSION

Records of members of the medical profession are often rather unsatisfactory from the point of view of the family historian though some publications do provide quite a lot of information. *The Medical Directory* has been published annually since 1845 (there was a separate *Directory* for Scotland from 1852 to 1860); it may contain details of the person's career and specialisations. *The Medical Register* first appeared in 1859 but gives briefer details.

A *List of Fellows of the Royal College of Surgeons of Edinburgh from 1581 to 1873* was published by the College in 1874. The Library of the Royal College of Surgeons at 18 Nicolson Street, Edinburgh EH8 9DW, has an extensive archive, with records on surgeons and chirurgeons going back to the beginning of the 16th century.

The Royal College of Physicians of Edinburgh Library at 9 Queen Street, Edinburgh EH2 1JQ, holds both primary sources and printed material.

In Glasgow, The Royal College of Physicians and Surgeons at 234 St. Vincent Street, Glasgow G2 5RJ, has college records and lists of fellows and members.

Some hospital records are held in NAS – class reference HH. There are also a number of local Health Board Archives, including Dumfries and Galloway at the Crichton Royal Hospital, the

Glasgow Health Board at the University of Glasgow, the Medical Archives Centre at Edinburgh University and Aberdeen Royal Infirmary, Aberdeen.

SEAMEN

Royal Navy

There are no official records for a Scottish navy and information on those who served in the Navy has therefore to be sought in the Public Record Office in London. *Naval Records for Genealogists*, by N.A.M. Rodger, provides a detailed guide to finding your way through these records.

Sailors on Merchant vessels

As with the Royal Navy, most of the official records for men serving on merchant vessels are in the Public Record Office in London. *My Ancestor was a Merchant Seaman*, by Christopher T. and Michael J. Watts, contains much useful information on locating records and there is a good bibliography.

The East India Company, in which many Scots served, had its own naval forces and these records are in the India Office Library (see page 170).

Scottish ships outward- and inward-bound carrying cargoes on which duty was payable, are listed in the Customs Accounts of each port which form part of the Exchequer records in NAS. Only the name of the master is given.

Cases concerning maritime cases (both civil and criminal) were heard in the Admiral's Court (sitting in Edinburgh) but Admirals

Depute held local courts. Unfortunately few records have survived. *Guide to the National Archives of Scotland* lists those that are in the NAS.

Trinity House of Leith was a mutual benefit society for poor and sick mariners and their families. GD226 is a collection of papers relating to this society, dealing with payments to seamen and their families, dating back to the 17th century.

TEACHERS & PUPILS

The responsibility for appointing teachers and schoolmasters usually rested with the parish or the burgh. In the parish, you may find references to these appointments and other dealings with the schoolmaster in the heritors' records, in the kirk session minutes or in the presbytery minutes. The local schoolmaster was very often the session clerk of the parish.

In the burghs, the duty of paying the schoolmaster was often divided between the burgh and the Kirk, resulting in many differences of opinion. Town council minutes contain frequent refer-

---

SSPCK SCHOOLS

The Society in Scotland for Propagating Christian Knowledge was formed in 1709 to build and maintain schools in parts of the Highlands and Islands where it was thought they were most needed. 'SSPCK Schoolmasters 1709–1872', edited by AS. Cowper, lists all those appointed and gives brief notes on their careers.

ences to the burgh schoolmasters – appointments, dismissals, fees paid by scholars and other matters. Check the repertories of the royal burghs.

There are several *Source Lists* of material in the NAS concerning schoolmasters and schools in the Archives, but the *Lists* are not indexed.

The organised training of teachers was not introduced until 1826 and after 1843 training colleges were run under the auspices of the Established, Free, Episcopal and Roman Catholic Churches. The two-volume *History of Scottish Education*, by James Scotland, gives a good account of the subject and includes notes on source material.

From 1872 onwards, responsibility for parish schools and the appointment of teachers passed to the school boards. Their records – minute books and school log books – are mostly with the district councils, though a few are in the National Archives of Scotland including those for Midlothian and East Lothian (class reference CO). Few names of pupils are given.

Reports of Inspectors of Schools date from 1896 and may name teachers – but not the pupils. These reports are in the NAS – class reference ED16-18.

Private Schools

From the 17th century onwards a number of schools – sometimes known as 'Hospitals' – were established by charitable trusts, among which were Heriot's Hospital, the Merchant Maidens' Hospital (later known as Mary Erskine's), George Watson's, Daniel Stewart's in Edinburgh, Hutcheson's in Glasgow and

Robert Gordon's in Aberdeen. Some of these and other private schools keep lists of former pupils with biographical notes on them. Records of George Heriot's School are held in the NAS (GD421).

University students & graduates

Many students went to university, attended some classes but did not graduate. Surviving records of both students and those who were awarded degrees are on the whole very unsatisfactory, both in the respective university archives or in printed lists, and with the exception of the Glasgow University matriculation rolls, provide little or no information of value to the family historian. In most cases, the details given are so sparse that it is impossible to determine the identity of the student. *The Matriculation Albums of the University of Glasgow 1728–1858*, edited by W. Innes Addison, in many cases give the name of the student's father and place of residence. A cross-reference is also given to other members of the same family who studied at the university.

APPENDIX 1   SOURCES FOR SCOTTISH FAMILY HISTORY

This is a guide to some classes of records which may be of use in tracing the history of a family. It is not comprehensive nor are all the classes of records under a particular section listed. Many records only cover a particular period, or refer to one class of person or district. Where records are shown to be printed, this may refer only to certain areas or certain periods of time.

KEY TO WHERE RECORDS CAN BE FOUND	
NAS	National Archives of Scotland
A	Archives (district or other)
L	Locally (libraries etc.)
P	Printed (some transcripts or abridgements)

Government Records

Parliamentary Reports: P Reports on a wide range of matters – education; emigration; the poor; working conditions; etc. Evidence heard and cases quoted.

Register of the Great Seal NAS; P Crown grants of land and major offices.

Register of the Privy Seal NAS; P Feudal casualties; minor commissions; remissions; legitimations.

Register of the Privy Council NAS; P Administrative and judicial business.

Court & Legal Records

Court of Session NAS Processes; productions; evidence and judgements in civil cases; register of deeds.

Protocol Books NAS; A; L; P Records of notaries recording deeds; bonds; sasines; contracts.

High Court of Justiciary NAS Processes; evidence and judgements in criminal cases.

Sheriffdoms NAS Civil and criminal cases; register of deeds; services of heirs; diligence records; miscellaneous material.

Burghs NAS; A; L; P Court books; council minutes; retours; registers of deeds; admission of burgesses; guildry records; protocol books; diligence records.

Commissary Court Testaments and inventories; edicts; deeds; processes; divorce.

Regality NAS; A Records of lands held by crown vassals; accounts; rentals; deeds; court books; hornings.

Stewartry & Bailiary NAS Records of lands administered on behalf of the crown; court records; deeds.

Baron Court NAS; A; L; P Court books (mainly keeping good neighbourhood); rentals.

Justices of the Peace NAS; A; L; P Local law and order; licensing; recruitment; roads and bridges.

Admiralty Court NAS Civil and criminal jurisdiction in maritime matters.

Financial Records

Exchequer Rolls   NAS   Payments to Crown of casualties, duties.

Hearth Tax   NAS; A; L; P   Tax on hearths c.1691.

Poll Tax   NAS; A; L; P   Tax on persons c. 1696.

Exchequer Records   NAS   18th century taxes on windows, dogs, etc.; import/export records; bounties.

Valuation Rolls   NAS; A; L; P   Annual valuations of property 1855 onwards; some earlier valuations.

Customs & Excise   NAS   Customs letter books; shipping registers.

Diligence Records   NAS; A; L   Cases of debt (see also Sheriff, Burgh and Regality records)

Forfeited Estate papers   NAS; P   Administration of forfeited estates after 1715 and 1745 rebellions – rentals; estate papers; etc.

Land Records

Registers of Sasines   NAS; A   General and Particular Registers of Sasines; Burgh Registers of Sasines; land transfer by inheritance, purchase or security for a loan.

Protocol Books   NAS; A; L; P   Early notaries' records of land transfer.

Register of Tailzies   NAS   Records of entails.

Retours   NAS; P   Services of heirs through Chancery (see also Sheriff Courts and Burghs).

Estate Papers   NAS; A; L; P   Charters, rentals, correspondence, estate accounts.

Church Records

Kirk Session NAS; A; L; P Disciplinary cases; testimonials; list of lairs; pew rents; communion rolls and parish listings; some baptisms, marriages and burials; payments to the poor.

Presbytery NAS; A; P Cases referred from Kirk Session; matters concerning the church.

Synod NAS; P Church administration; some disciplinary cases.

General Assembly NAS Admission of new ministers; disputed calls; 18th century lists of Catholics; general matters.

Dissenting Churches NAS; A; L Kirk Session, Presbytery and Synod – as for Church of Scotland.

Heritors Minutes NAS; A; L Upkeep of the church, manse and school; relief of the poor.

APPENDIX 2 CLASSES OF RECORDS IN THE NATIONAL ARCHIVES OF SCOTLAND

This list covers the classes of record in the National Archives of
Scotland that are most likely to be of value in studying Scottish
family history. The content of the various classes is discussed in
relevant chapters.

AC Admiralty Court Mercantile and maritime cases; court
books; criminal proceedings; contracts, piracy and mutiny.

AD Lord Advocate's Records Precognitions (mainly after 1812)
for more serious crimes; procedure books.

AF Agriculture & Fisheries for Scotland Records of Royal
Commission on Highlands & Islands 1883; emigration to
Canada 1886–89; agricultural statistics 1866 onwards; fisheries.

B Burghs (Royal Burghs) Court Books; Town Council
Minutes,; sasines; deeds.

BR British Rail (Scotland)

C Chancery Retours (services of heirs); Charters given under
the Great Seal.

CC Commissary Court Testaments; edicts of executry; processes; inventories; divorce (Edinburgh court only).

CE Customs & Excise Records of customs officers.

CH1 General Assembly Papers

CH2 Records of the Church of Scotland Kirk Session,
Presbytery, Synod papers.

CH3 Records of Dissenting Churches Kirk Session, Presbytery
and Synod.

CH10 Quaker Records

CH11 Methodist Records

CH12 Episcopal Records

CH13 United Free Church Records

CO County Council Records Town and country planning; taxation; cess rolls; some valuation rolls; upkeep of roads; parochial board business; water and lighting; school board records.

CS Court of Session Register of Deeds; processes, court cases.

DI Diligence Records Court matters mainly concerning debt.

E Exchequer and Treasury Forfeited estate papers; taxation; trade; 17th-century army muster rolls.

ED Education Department of Scotland Reports of Inspectors of Schools (19th century).

GD Gifts and Deposits Family and business papers on loan or gifted to the NAS.

HD Highland Destitution Accounts; letter books; records of Highland Emigration Society (mid-19th century).

HR Heritors' Records JC High Court of Justiciary

JP Justices of the Peace Courts

NP Notarial Records Protocol books (mainly 16th and 17th century); admission of notaries.

NRA National Register of Archives Repertories of collections of papers and archives surveyed but not in the NAS.

OS Ordnance Survey List of place names.

PC Privy Council

PS Privy Seal

RD Register of Deeds Books of Council and Session.

RH Register House Papers A large collection of papers on a
wide range of topics, including Local Records (records of
Baronies, Regalities, Stewartries and Bailiaries) RH11; a collection of Genealogies RH16, and Roman Catholic Registers
RH21.

RHP Register House Plans

RS Register of Sasines General Registers and Particular
Registers.

RT Register of Tailzies Records of entailed estates.

SC Sheriff Courts

VR Valuation Rolls

APPENDIX 3 GLOSSARY

The glossary that follows explains some of the words commonly found in 17th- and 18th-century source material. Latin words or phrases are included only if they are often found in vernacular documents.

Several dictionaries can be consulted for more information:

Chambers Twentieth Century Dictionary Various one-volume editions; unexpectedly useful for Scots words.

Concise Scots Dictionary edited by Mairi Robinson A useful reference book, but because of its size it cannot include everything.

The Scottish National Dictionary edited by W. Grant & D. Murison 10 volumes or in compact two-volume edition.

Jamieson's Dictionary of the Scottish Language A large work in several volumes which can be consulted in libraries. Check entries given in more than one dictionary, as the examples quoted of the use of words or phrases may vary and interpretations differ.

Dictionary of the Older Scottish Tongue edited by W.A. Craigie, A.J. Aitken & J. Stevenson A work in many volumes, still being compiled, but the best place to look up old Scots words and phrases.

Glossary of Scottish Legal Terms by A.D. Gibb A useful guide to words and terms found in legal documents.

Formulary of Old Scots Legal Documents by Peter Gouldesbrough This includes examples of various kinds of legal documents and is an excellent aid to understanding the form and phraseology used in such material.

act formal decision

abulziements clothing, personal possessions

addettit indebted, owing

advocation appeal to a higher court; patronage of church, benefice

agnate persons related through the father

air, ayr heir

airschip inheritance; see heirship

aitts oats

alienate sell

allenarly only

als as or also

anent with reference to, concerning

annalzie alienate

annexes and connexes appurtenances of property

annual rent interest on money lent

apparent heir one who will be the heir but who has not completed his title. (NB: heir apparent is the person who will succeed X if he survives him.)

apprising sheriff's sentence by which debtor had to sell heritable rights to pay appriser

apud acta at the time of the proceedings

arles earnest, evidence of engagement of a servant

arrage (harrage) labour services due from a tenant

assedation lease

assignation assigning of rights

assize jury; articles subject to a regulation or tax

assoilzie decide in favour of defender; acquit

astrict tie lands to a mill where all grain on those lands must be ground at that mill

attour besides

aucht (number) eight

auchtand owing

aumbry cupboard

avail value

awand owing

awin own

bailliary, bailyerie office or authority of a bailie; the area under the jurisdiction of a bailie

bailie, baillie one acting for the person granting sasine; an officer in a barony; an official in a Burgh

bairns' pairt part of a parent's moveable estate to which child or children are entitled on death of parent – one-third if the other parent is still living, one half in other cases

barony lands of a baron who held of the Crown with certain rights of jurisdiction

baxter baker

be by

beltane Whitsunday – 15 May

bere, bear, beir barley

bigging building

birlayman a trusted person appointed to give verdicts in the Barony Court, and to make assessments for Burgh Courts

blenche ferme nominal rent

Bond/band written legal agreement to repay money

boll measure of grain

books of adjournal records of the Justiciary Court

bot without

bounteth, bounty gratuity added to servant's fee

bowing a system by which a herd was let out for grazing

breid bread

brieve, breve official letter or warrant of Chancery authorising an inquest in a particular matter: a writ

broyer brother

bruik have the use of

burd board

but without

by and attour besides

bygane: bygone past

byrun past

capital pleas cases such as murder, robbery, rape and fire-raising, heard only in the High Court of Justiciary

capon fowl

carriage service of carting goods over a short or long distance demanded from tenants by the superior

casualty payment to a superior on an event the occurrence of which cannot be predicted, such as nonentrie

cautioner one acting as a surety

cayne, cain rent paid in kind

cess land tax

chalder measure for grain, malt, lime, etc.

charter deed granted by superior

chopin liquid measure

clachan small settlement

clare constat (precept of) document recognising the claim of an heir to inherit and be infeft

cobill small boat

cognate relative through the mother

commonty common pasture land

commutation money equivalent of rent paid in kind or in service

compear, compeir appear in an action

comprising process whereby land might be taken for debt

compt account

confirmation recognition of due appointment of executors, ratification of right of purchaser of land by the superior

conjunctlie and severallie jointly and by each one, obligation whereby each party is liable to perform whole obligation

conjunct fee joint holding by husband and wife

cordiner shoemaker

cottar one holding land in return for labour service

cottoun settlement occupied by cottars

cruives fish traps

cupill rafter (of a roof)

dale, daill plank, timbers

decern to decide judicially, to decree

decree final judgement

decreet, decreit decision or judgement

demit dismiss, discharge

dempster officer pronouncing judgement

depone to give evidence

deposition evidence on oath

depredation stealing of cattle

destination direction as to those who are to succeed to property

diet date for court hearing

dilate, dilait to accuse, inform against

dispone convey land

disposition deed by which heritable or moveable property is conveyed to another

dittay matter of criminal charge, indictment

divot turf

domicile usual residence

domicills household goods

effeiring to belonging or relating to

eik addition, codicil

ell standard length – usually of cloth

entres interest

escheat, escheit forfeiture of property (moveable or heritable)

evident document establishing legal title

exerce to carry out official duties

exoner exonerate; relieve

factory deed empowering one to act for another

failzie failure; non-fulfilment

farder further

farmtoun settlement (arable and pasture land and dwellings)

fauld enclosed cultivated piece of land

feal, faill turf

fee full right of property (as against liferent); payment to servant

fencible soldier called up for home service

ferd fourth

ferme, ferm rent, annual payment

feu feudal holding

feu ferme rent due under feu charter

feuar, fiar one who holds a fee (not a tenant)

fiars price fixed for grain each year in each county on which stipends were calculated

firlot measure of grain, a quarter of a boll

fleschour flesher, butcher

fodder often used to refer to straw

foirfaltour forfeiture

forenamit previously mentioned

forestall to buy goods on the way to market

forrow cow cow not in calf

forsamekle forasmuch

freeman, freman one having freedom of a burgh, a burgess

freith free

fulzie dung

furth beyond, outside

gart caused

gear moveable goods

german full (of a brother or sister or, occasionally, cousin)

gif, gyf if, whether

gild brother member of a guild

glebe land allocated to a minister in the parish

grassum single payment made on entry to lease or feu or on renewal of a lease

graith gear, equipment

gudschir, guidsire grandfather

guid-father father-in-law

guids goods

haill whole

hairst harvest

handfast to be betrothed

head-dyke boundary dyke

heirship (moveables) the best goods taken by heir by right to furnish his property

herezeld duty – usually a beast – due to a landlord on the death of the tenant

heritage property consisting of land and houses

heritor landowner – usually referring to one who contributed to upkeep of church

hind farm servant, ploughman

hog pig or an unshorn yearling lamb

horning penal diligence for debt, an order to the debtor to pay

husbandland holding of a husbandman (originally 26 Scots acres)

ilkane, ilke each, every one

impignorat pledge

incontinent immediately

indictment written charge of crime, summons

indweller inhabitant of a town which was not a burgh, resident without burgess rights in a burgh

infeft to put person in heritable possession of land

infield land constantly cultivated

inhibition writ forbidding a debtor selling or burdening his property before claims of creditor are settled

inquest a body of people summoned to examine such matters as a service of heirs

insicht (and plenishing) household furniture

instrument legal document given on completion of legal act such as sasine

interdict judicial prohibition

intromet with deal with (funds or property)

intromission transaction concerning money

inventar inventory of moveable property

ish, ische expiry, exit

joyse enjoy

jus mariti a husband's right to his wife's moveables

jus relictae a widow's right to one-third or one-half of her husband's property on his death

kain (cain) customary payments from tenants – usually in kind

ken, kend know, known

kindly tenants holders of lands having a kind of hereditary right to them

kirklands lands of which an ecclesiastical body was the superior

kist chest

knaveship a measure of grain paid to the miller's servant for work done at the mill

kye cows

lade mill-stream

laich, laigh low

lair grave or burial plot

Lammas 1 August

landward part of parish which is in the country, outside a town

latterwill a person's wishes for disposal of property after death, will

lead to transport grain, coal, etc.

lesum, liesum permissible, right or proper

letters court writ or warrant

libel declaration in a summons; charge (in the legal sense); as a verb very commonly in the phrase 'as libelled', that is, as described in the summons

liberties trade precinct of a burgh

liferent property held during a person's lifetime only

liquidat expenses fixed expenses

litster dyer

lousit released

lykeas as

mail, maill rent

mailing land for which rent is paid

mains home farm on an estate

mair more

mak(e) faith testify on oath

mart carcase of animal slaughtered at Martinmas, animal due to be given up by tenant at Martinmas

Martinmas, Mertinmas 11 November – term day

meadow grassland mowed for hay

meikill much, large

meith boundary or to fix a boundary

meliorat improved

merk, mark old Scots silver coin worth 13s. 4d. Scots (about 1s. 2d. sterling)

merkland measure of land for which duty paid was one merk

messuage principal dwelling house within a barony

minor usually a young person between 12 and 21 (female) or 14 and 21 (male); can be used generally for anyone under 21

mortcloth cloth used to cover the coffin

mortification grant made to institution – usually ecclesiastical

moss place where peats are cut

moveable estate property which is not heritable (personal possessions not land) *muir* hill pasture

multures grain given to miller of mill to which a person was bound

mutchkin liquid measure

nolt cattle

nonage minority

nonentry casualty caused by death of a vassal payable till entry of new heir

notar, notary one licensed to record legal transactions

novodamus charter altering terms of earlier charter

nowt cattle

numerat paid in cash

obligatione legal agreement to pay a sum of money to another

omissa things omitted from executry

outfield land which was not cropped continuously

outsets small piece of land detached from or outlying from main holding but dependent on it

overheid in total

oversman one who decides if the arbiters differ

oxgate, oxgang measure of land (based on the amount an ox could plough in a day)

oy grandchild

panel the prisoner

pari passu share and share alike

paroch, parochin parish

peck measure of corn, oats, etc.

pendicle small piece of ground

persew prosecute

pertein, pertain to belong to

pertinents *(as in parts, pertinents & pendicles)* everything making up part of lands conveyed

(the) piece each

pirn spool or reel for thread

plenishing furnishings

ploughgate division of arable land, eight oxgates

poind, poynd to seize and sell goods of a debtor

portioner owner of small estate or piece of land

precept warrant or authority granted by superior for owner or heir's infeftment

precognition statement of witness (taken before the proceedings)

premiss term (in a document)

premonition official warning

pro indiviso undivided

process legal documents relating to all steps of a case

procurator lawyer or agent

propone to state in a law court

proport purport, convey

protest legal demand for payment of money owing

pupil children up to 12 (girls) and 14 (boys)

quha who

quheit wheat

quhilk which

quhyt free, clear

quit-claim relinquish claim or title

quoad sacra parish disjoined for ecclesiastical purposes only

quot tax on estate of deceased due to Commissaries (one-twentieth)

ratification confirmation

reduce to annul

regrate to buy food in a market and re-sell in the same market or one within four miles

relict widow

relief sum paid by heir on entering as new vassal to superior

reset crime of receiving stolen property known to be stolen

resignation vassal gives up estate to superior

rests arrears

retour extract from Chancery of service of an heir to ancestor

reversion obligation by creditor under which the debtor may redeem estate given as security for loan on repayment of loan

rig strip of cultivated land

roods measure of land, land belonging to a burgh rented or feued for cultivation and building

rolls list of cases to be heard

roume, room piece of rented land

roup auction

runrig strips of land allocated to tenants

samen, samyn same

sasine, seisin infeftment; act of giving legal possession of land

scaithe, skaith harm, damage

scandal slander

secluding excluding

sederunt meeting, minutes listing those present

sensyne since

sequels meal perquisite of mill servant

sequestration bankruptcy

services of free tenants services demanded of tenants by landlord such as assistance at harvest *set (sett)* let

shielings summer pastures on high ground

siclyk, sicklyk likewise

skaith harm

soume sum

souming, sowming action to determine how many cattle might be grazed on certain area of pasture

sovertie surety

spuilzie plunder

statute labour so many days' work on roads demanded from tenants, cottars and labourers

steading farm buildings, originally the farm itself

steelbow, steilbow grant by landlord of grain, cattle, tools, etc. to tenant, to be returned by the tenant at the end of the lease

stent assessment, tax

sucken obligation to use a certain mill

summa total

superior one who makes a grant of land to another who is then his vassal and pays feu-duty

tack lease

tacksman holder of a lease – usually a substantial tenant

tailzie entail

take instruments make a written notarial record

teind tenth part of produce of land paid to the church

tenement block of flats

terce liferent of one-third of her husband's heritage given by law to a widow

term date when interest or rent is payable

thir these

thirlage binding of tenant to grind his grain at a particular mill on the estate

tidy (tydie) cow a cow in calf, a cow giving milk

tocher dowry, marriage portion

toft cultivated ground attached to a house

toun settlement

translation deed in which the assignee of a debt conveys it to a third party

tutor guardian of children who were in pupillarity (see *pupil*)

umquhile deceased; the late

ut supra as above

utencils and domiciles personal possessions, household goods

uterine having the same mother (of a half-brother or -sister)

vassal one who holds land from a superior under feudal law

vest to endow, secure

victuall food, provisions

wadset pledge of lands (conveyed by sasine) but with right of recovery on repayment of money borrowed

ward guardianship of an infant heir with control of lands belonging to the superior during minory of the heir; also form of feudal tenure in return for military service

warrandice guarantee that right conveyed shall be effected

warrant original document of which a copy is made for a register

warning formal notice to tenant to remove within 40 days

waulk mill fulling mill

webster, wobster weaver

wedder male sheep bred for fleece and meat

Whitsunday 15 May – term day

winning digging up (of peats)

wright carpenter
writ a writing having legal significance
writer a lawyer
yett gate
yrto thereto

APPENDIX 4 USEFUL ADDRESSES

Scottish Family History Societies

Contact addresses may change when a new secretary is appointed. The local public library will probably be able to give you the new address. In addition to the family history societies listed below, there are many local history societies which are also concerned with family history. Consult a local librarian for information.

Aberdeen and North East of Scotland Family History Society Aberdeen Family History Centre, 164 King Street, Aberdeen AB24 5BD

Alloway & Southern Ayrshire Family History Society c/o Alloway Public Library, Doonholm Road, Alloway, Ayr KA7 4QQ

Anglo Scottish Family History Society Clayton House, 59 Piccadilly, Manchester MR1 2AQ

Borders Family History Society 15 Edinburgh Road, Greenlaw, Berwickshire TD10 6XF

Central Scotland Family History Society 4 Fir Lane, Larbert, Stirlingshire FK5 3LW

Dumfries and Galloway Family History Society Family History Centre, 9 Glasgow Street, Dumfries DG2 9AF

East Ayrshire Family History Society c/o The Dick Institute, Elmbank Ave., Kilmarnock KA1 3BU

Fife Family History Society 30 Duddingston Drive, Kirkcaldy, Fife KY2 6JP

Glasgow and West of Scotland Family History Society Unit 5, 22 Mansfield Street, Glasgow G11 5QP

Highland Family History Society c/o Reference Room, Public Library, Farraline Park, Inverness IV1 1NH

Lanarkshire Family History Society c/o Hamilton Central Library, 98 Cadzow Street, Hamilton ML3 6HQ

Largs & North Ayrshire Family History Society 2 Raillies Road, Largs, Ayrshire KA30 8QZ

Lothians Family History Society c/o Lasswade High School Centre, Eskdale Drive, Bonnyrigg, Midlothian EH19 2LA

Orkney Family History Society 26 Royal Oak Road, Kirkwall KW15 1RF

Renfrewshire Family History Society Linn House, Linn Park Gardens, Johnstone PA5 8LH

Scottish Genealogy Society Library and Family History Centre, 15 Victoria Terrace, Edinburgh EH1 2JL

Shetland Family History Society 6 Hillhead, Lerwick ZE1 OED

Tay Valley Family History Society Family History Research Centre, 179 Princes Street, Dundee DD4 6DQ

Troon and District Family History Society Troon Public Library, South Beach, Troon, Ayrshire KA10 6EF

Record Repositories

These are some of Scotland's main archives and libraries, arranged by local authority district, which you may wish to visit. There are also others with specialised or very localised interests. Before visiting it is wise to check opening hours by telephone. Not all are open every day and for some you may need to book a seat as space is limited. In most cases, there is no fees.

There is more information on Scottish libraries and archives in: *British Archives* by Janet Foster & Julia Sheppard; *Exploring Scottish History* ed. Michael Cox; and *Data Sheets* issued by the Scottish Records Association

Aberdeen & Aberdeenshire
Aberdeen City Archives, Town House, Broad St, Aberdeen AB10 1AQ; tel 01224 522513 fax 01224 522491

Aberdeen City Archives, Old Aberdeen Branch (for former counties of Aberdeen, Banff, Kincardine and Moray and some City of Aberdeen), Old Aberdeen House, Dunbar Street, Aberdeen AB24 1UE; tel 01224 481775 fax 01224 495830

Aberdeen University Library, Dept. of Special Collections & Archives, Kings College, Aberdeen AB24 3SW; tel 01224 272598

Northern Health Services Archives, ARI Woolmanhill, Aberdeen AB25 1LD; tel 01224 633123

Angus
Angus Archives, Montrose Library, 214 High St, Montrose DD10 8PH; tel 01674 671415 fax 01674 671810

Argyll & Bute
Argyll & Bute Council Archives, Manse Brae, Lochgilphead, Argyll PA31 8QU; tel 01546 604120 fax 01546 606897

Ayrshire
Ayrshire Archives Centre, Craigie Estate, Ayr KA8 0SS; tel 01292 287584 fax 10292 284918

Clackmannan
Clackmannshire Council Archives, 26-28 Drysdale St, Alloa FK10 1JL; tel 01259 722262 fax 01259 219469

Dumfries & Galloway
Archive Centre, 33 Burns St, Dumfries DG1 2PS; tel 01387 264126 fax 01387 269254

Ewart Library, Catherine St, Dumfries DG1 1JB; tel 01387 253820

Dumfries Health Board, Crichton Museum, Easterbrook Hall, Dumfries DG1 4TG; tel 01387 244360

Dundee
Dundee City Archive and Record Centre, 21 City Sq., Dundee DD1 3BY; tel 01382 434494

Dundee University Archives, The University, Dundee DD1 4HN; tel 01382 344095

Edinburgh
City of Edinburgh Council Archives; City Chambers, High St, Edinburgh EH1 1YJ; tel 0131 529 4616 fax 0131 529 4957

National Archives of Scotland, HM General Register House, Edinburgh EH1 3YY; tel general enquiries 0131 5351360; research enquiries 0131 5351328

General Register Office for Scotland, New Register House, Edinburgh EH1 3YT; tel 0131 3340380 fax 0131 3144400

Edinburgh University Archives, George Sq., Edinburgh EH8 9LJ; tel 0131 6503384

Court of the Lord Lyon, New Register House, Edinburgh EH1 3YT; tel 0131 5567255 fax 0131 5572148

National Library of Scotland, George IV Bridge, Edinburgh EH1 1EW; tel 0131 2264531 fax 0131 2206662

National Library of Scotland Map Library, 33 Salisbury Pl., Edinburgh EH9 1SL; tel 0131 2264531

Edinburgh Central Library, George IV Bridge, Edinburgh EH1 1EG; tel 0131 2255584

National Monuments Record of Scotland, Royal Commission on Ancient and Historic Monuments of Scotland, 16 Bernard Terr., Edinburgh EH8 9NX; tel 0131 6621456

Lothian Health Board, Medical Archives Centre, Edinburgh University Library, George Sq., Edinburgh EH8 9LJ; tel 0131 6503392 fax 0131 6506863

Royal College of Surgeons of Edinburgh, 18 Nicolson St, Edinburgh EH8 9DW; tel 0131 5271600 fax 0131 5576406

Royal College of Physicians of Edinburgh, 9 Queen St, Edinburgh EH2 1JQ; tel 0131 2257324

Scottish Catholic Archives, 16 Drummond Pl., Edinburgh EH3 6PL; tel 0131 5563661

Free Church of Scotland College, The Mound, Edinburgh EH1 2LS; tel 0131 2264978

Scottish United Services Museum, The Castle, Edinburgh EH1 2NG; tel 0131 2257534

Falkirk

Falkirk History Research Centre, Falkirk Museum, Callendar
House, Callendar Park, Falkirk FK1 1YR; tel 01324 503770
fax 01324 503771

Fife

Fife Council, Fife House, North St, Glenrothes, KY7 5LT; tel
01592 414141

St Andrews University Library, Dept. of Manuscripts, North St,
St Andrews, KY16 9TR; tel 01334 476161

Dunfermline District Libraries, 1 Abbot St, Dunfermline KY12
7NW; tel 01383 312600

Kirkcaldy District Libraries, War Memorial Gardens, Kirkcaldy
KY1 1YG; tel 01592 412878

Glasgow

Glasgow City Archives, Mitchell Library, North St., Glasgow G3
7DN; tel 0141 287 2999

Glasgow University Archives & Business Record Centre, 13
Thurso St, Glasgow G11 6PE; tel 0141 330 5516 fax 1041
3304158

Greater Glasgow Health Board Archive, Glasgow University
Archives, 77-81 Dumbarton Road, Glasgow G11 6PW; tel
0141 330 5516 fax 0141 3304158

Royal College of Physicians & Surgeons of Glasgow, 234–242 St
Vincent St, Glasgow G2 4RJ; tel 0141 2216072 fax 0141
2211804

Scottish Jewish Archive Centre, Garnethill Synagogue, 125–7 Hill
St, Glasgow G3 6UB; tel 0141 3324911

Archdiocese of Glasgow, 196 Clyde St, Glasgow G1; tel 0141 2265898

Highland
Highland Council Archive, The Library, Farraline Park, Inverness IV1 1NH; tel 01463 220330: Fax: 01463 711128

Clan Donald Lands Trust, Armadale, Sleat, Isle of Skye IV45 8RS; tel 01471 844389

Midlothian
Midlothian Council Archives, Library Headquarters, 2 Clerk St, Loanhead, Midlothian EH20 9DR; tel 0131 270 7500 fax 0131 440 4635

Moray
Moray Council Heritage Centre, Grant Lodge, Cooper Park, Elgin, Moray IV30 1HS; tel 01343 563413

North Highlands
North Highland Archive, Wick Library, Sinclair Terr., Wick KW1 5AB; tel 01955 606432 fax 01955 603000

North Lanarkshire
North Lanarkshire Archive, 10 Kelvin Rd, Lenziemill, Cumbernauld G67 2BA; tel 01236 737114

Orkney
Orkney Archives, Orkney Library, Laing St, Kirkwall, KW15 1NW; tel 01856 873166 fax 01856 875260

Perth & Kinross
Perth & Kinross Council Archive, AK Bell Library, 2–8 York Pl., Perth, PH2 8EP; tel 01738 477022 fax 01738 477010

Scottish Borders
Scottish Borders Archive & Local History Centre, St. Mary's Mill, Selkirk TD7 5EW; tel 01750 20842 fax 01750 22875

Shetland
Shetland Archives, 44 King Harald St, Lerwick ZE1 OEQ; tel 01595 696247 fax 01595 696533

South Lanarkshire
South Lanarkshire Council Archives and Information, Management Service, 30 Hawbank Rd, College Milton, East Kilbride G74 5EX; tel 01355 239193

Stirling
Stirling Council Archives Services, Unit 6, Burghmuir Industrial Estate, Stirling FK7 7PY; tel 01786 450745

West Lothian
West Lothian Council Archives, 7 Rutherford Sq., Brucefield Industrial Estate, Livingston, West Lothian EH54 9BU; tel 01506 460020 fax 01506 416167

APPENDIX 5 SELECT BIBLIOGRAPHY

Adamson, Duncan *West Lothian Hearth Tax 1691* Scottish Record Society 1981

Addison, WI *Matriculation Albums of the University of Glasgow 1728-1858* Maclehose 1913

Bell, George *Dictionary and Digest of the Law of Scotland* (7th edn) Edinburgh 1890

Black, George F *The Surnames of Scotland* New York Public Library, reprinted 1974

Bloxham, Ben *Key to the Parochial Registers of Scotland* Brigham Young University Press, USA 1970

Brunton G & Haig D *Senators of the College of Justice 1532-1850* Edinburgh n.d

Couper, WJ *The Reformed Presbyterian Church in Scotland, its Congregations, Ministers and Students* UF Church of Scotland 1925

Cowper, AS *SSPCK Schoolmasters 1709-1872* Scottish Record Society 1997

Cox, Michael *Exploring Scottish History* 2nd edition SLA, SLHF and SRA 1999

Ewing, W *Annals of the Free Church of Scotland 1843-1900* Edinburgh 1914

Ferguson, JPS *Directory of Scottish Newspapers* National Library of Scotland 1984

Ferguson, JPS *Scottish Family Histories* National Library of Scotland 1986

Foster, J & Sheppard, J*British Archives – A Guide to Archive Resources in the United Kingdom* London 1984

Fowler, Simon *Army Records for Family Historians* PRO 1992

Fowler, Simon, Spencer, W & Tamblin, S *Army Service Records of the First World War* PRO 1997

Gandy, Michael *Catholic Missions and Registers 1700-1880* Gandy 1993

Gibb, Andrew Dewar *Students' Glossary of Scottish Legal Terms* Edinburgh 1946

Gibson, J & Medlycott M *Militia Lists and Musters 1757-1876* FFHS 3rd edn 1994

Ginsburg, Madeleine *Victorian Dress in Photographs* London 1988

Gouldesbrough, Peter *Formulary of Old Scots Legal Documents* Stair Society 1985

Grant, Sir FJ *The Faculty of Advocates in Scotland 1532-1943* Scottish Record Society 1944

Groome, Francis *Ordnance Gazetteer of Scotland* Edinburgh 1882-5

Haythornthwaite, JA *Scotland in the Nineteenth Century – An Analytical Bibliography of Material relating to Scotland in Parliamentary Papers 1800-1900* Scolar Press 1993

Holding, Norman *The Location of British Army Records 1914-1918* FFHS 1991

Holding, Norman *World War I Army Ancestry* FFHS 1991

Irvine, Sherry *Your Scottish Ancestry – A Guide for North Americans* Salt Lake City, USA 1997

Lamb, JA *The Fasti of the United Free Church of Scotland 1900-1929* Edinburgh 1956

List & Index Society *Scottish Record Office Court of Session Productions c.1760-1840* List & Index Society 1987

MacConghail, Maire & Gorry, P *Tracing Irish Ancestors* Glasgow 1997

MacDougall, Ian *A Catalogue of Labour Records in Scotland* Scottish Labour History Society 1978

MacKelvie, W *Annals and Statistics of the United Presbyterian Church* Edinburgh 1873

McKechnie, Hector *The Society of Writers to H.M. Signet* Edinburgh 1936

Moir DG *The Early Maps of Scotland to 1850 (2 vols.)* Royal Scottish Geographical Society 1973 & 1983

Oliver, George*Photographs and Local History* London 1989

Payne, Peter L *Studies in Scottish Business History* London 1967

Polls, Robert *Dating Old Photographs* FFHS 1992

Pryde, George Smith *The Burghs of Scotland – A Critical List* OUP 1965

Rodger, NAM *Naval Records for Genealogists* PRO 1984

Scotland, James *The History of Scottish Education (2 vols)* London 1969

Scott, Hew *Fasti Ecclesiae Scoticanae* reprinted Edinburgh 1961

Sinclair, Cecil *Tracing Scottish Local History in the Scottish Record Office* HMSO 1994

Sinclair, Cecil *Tracing Your Scottish Ancestors in the Scottish Record Office* HMSO 1990

Small, R *History of the Congregations of the United Presbyterian Church 1733-1900* Edinburgh 1904

Stair Society *Guide to the National Archives of Scotland* Stair Society & HMSO 1996

Steel, DJ *Sources for Scottish Genealogy and Family History* London 1970

Stevenson, D & WB *Scottish Texts and Calendars – an Analytical*

Guide to Serial Publications Scottish History Society 1987

Stuart, Margaret & Paul, Sir JB *Scottish Family History* reprinted Baltimore, USA 1978

Timperley, Loretta R *A Directory of Landownership in Scotland c.1770* Scottish Record Society 1976

Torrance, DR *Scottish Trades and Professions – a Selected Bibliography* SAFHS 1998

Watt, DER *Fasti Ecclesiae Scoticanae Medii Aevi* Scottish Record Society 1969

Watts, MJ & CT *My Ancestor was in the British Army* Society of Genealogists 1992

Watts, MJ & CT *My Ancestor was a Merchant Seaman* Society of Genealogists reprinted 1991

Willsher, Betty *Understanding Scottish Graveyards* Edinburgh 1985

Wise, T & S *Guide to Military Museums* Knighton, Powys 1994

APPENDIX 6 LIST OF OLD PARISHES IN SCOTLAND WITH UNITARY AUTHORITY, SHERIFF COURT & COMMISSARY COURT

The parishes in the list following are the old parishes, part of the civil administration of Scotland in the 17th, 18th and most of the 19th century; the parish name is often used in legal documents to identify a place. Over the years parishes were amalgamated and, for this reason, those researching in earlier periods will come across parishes which are not on this list. During the 19th century, as populations grew in various parts of the country, but particularly in central Scotland, the Church of Scotland created what are known as *quoad sacra* parishes to make it easier for ministers to serve their parishioners. A few such parishes which have registers before 1855, are included on this list and marked 'QS'. It should also be noted that, in certain parts of the country, and particularly in Perthshire, parishes could have several parts which were geographically separate from one another.

KEY TO COLUMN HEADINGS

Number the number given to the Old Parish Register. The same number – in most cases – is also used for census schedules of that district and also for the statutory registers (post-1854), though there have been some changes in the case of large cities and in more modern times.

County indicates, for the years prior to 1975, the county in which the parish was situated. The County (or Sheriffdom) is used in many historical documents to identify places and, for example, the Register of Sasines is arranged by these counties.

Local Authority indicates the authority which took responsibility for local government in the area in April 1996 and so has a statutory responsibility for local archives. Local authority and old parish boundaries do not always coincide but the name is given of the authority most likely to be responsible for keeping records. In some cases, an old parish is split between two authorities. In these cases, both authorities are given.

Sheriff Court in most cases, the main court of the county; it will have a register of deeds, inventories and wills. In Argyll, it is wise to check the repertories of both Dunoon and Inveraray Sheriff Courts.

Commissary Courts up to about 1823, these had responsibility for recording testaments and appointing executors. In some cases a testament may be found recorded in an adjoining commissariot – for example, it may be wise to search Glasgow as well as Hamilton and Campsie. After 1823, the business of the Commissary Courts was taken over by the Sheriff Courts and the Sheriff Court named is that most likely to contain Commissary records. In some cases there was more than one Sheriff Court in a county and useful information may be found in the records of these additional courts.

Note:

- Commissary records for Dundee 1823–32 are in Forfar Sheriff Court
- Commissary records for East Lothian and West Lothian 1823–30 are in Edinburgh Sheriff Court.

Parish	No.	County
Abbey	559	Renfrewshire
Abbey St Bathans	726	Berwickshire
Abbotshall	399	Fife
Abdie	400	Fife
Abercorn	661	W. Lothian (Linlithgowshire)
Aberdalgie	323	Perthshire
Aberdeen	168a	Aberdeenshire
Aberdour, Aberdeenshire	169	Aberdeenshire
Aberdour, Fife	401	Fife
Aberfoyle	325	Perthshire
Aberlady	702	E. Lothian (Haddingtonshire)
Aberlemno	269	Angus (Forfarshire)
Aberlour	145	Banffshire
Abernethy	326	Perthshire
Abernethy & Kincardine	90a	Invernessshire
Abernyte	327	Perthshire
Abertarff (see Boleskine)	92	Invernessshire
Aboyne	170	Aberdeenshire
Airlie	270	Angus (Forfarshire)
Airth	469	Stirlingshire
Alford	171	Aberdeenshire
Alloa	465	Clackmannanshire
Alness	57	Ross & Cromarty
Alva	470	Clackmannanshire (Stirlings. c.1600-1832)
Alvah	146	Banffshire
Alves	125	Morayshire (Elginshire)
Alvie	90b	Invernessshire
Alyth	328	Perthshire
Ancrum	780	Roxburghshire

Local Authority	Sheriff Court	Commissary Court
Renfrewshire	Paisley SC58	Glasgow CC9
The Scottish Borders	Duns SC60	Lauder CC15
Fife	Cupar SC20	St Andrews CC20
Fife	Cupar SC20	St Andrews CC20
W. Lothian	Linlithgow SC41	Dunkeld CC7
Perthshire	Perth SC49	Dunkeld CC7
Aberdeen City	Aberdeen SC1	Aberdeen CC1
Aberdeenshire	Aberdeen SC1	AberdeenCC1
Fife	Cupar SC20	Dunkeld CC7
Stirling	Perth SC49	Dunblane CC6
E. Lothian	Haddington SC40	Dunkeld CC7
Angus	Forfar SC47	St Andrews CC20
Moray	Banff SC2	Moray CC16
Perthshire	Perth SC49	Dunblane CC6
Highland	Inverness SC29	Inverness CC11
Perthshire	Perth SC49	Dunkeld CC7
Highland	Inverness SC29	Inverness CC11
Aberdeenshire	Aberdeen SC1	Aberdeen CC1
Angus	Forfar SC47	St Andrews CC20
Falkirk	Stirling SC67	Stirling CC21
Aberdeenshire	Aberdeen SC1	Aberdeen CC1
Clackmannan	Alloa SC64	Stirling CC21
Highland	Dingwall SC25	Ross CC19
Clackmannan	Alloa SC64	Stirling CC21
Aberdeenshire	Banff SC2	Aberdeen CC1
Moray	Elgin SC26	Moray CC16
Highland	Inverness SC29	Inverness CC11
Perthshire	Perth SC49	Dunkeld CC7
The Scottish Borders	Jedburgh SC62	Peebles CC18

Parish	No.	County
Annan	812	Dumfriesshire
Anstruther – Easter	402	Fife
Anstruther – Wester	403	Fife
Anwoth	855	Kircudbrightshire
Appin (see Lismore & Appin)	525	Argyll
Applecross (incl. Shieldaig & Kishorn)	58	Ross & Cromarty
Applegarth & Sibbaldbie	813a	Dumfriesshire
Arbirlot	271	Angus (Forfarshire)
Arbroath	272	Angus (Forfarshire)
Arbuthnott	250	Kincardineshire
Ardchattan (Balivodan)	504	Argyll
Ardclach	120	Nairnshire
Ardersier	91	Invernessshire
Ardnamurchan (incl Acharacle, Arisaig & Strontian [Islandfinnan])	505	Argyll
Ardrossan	576	Ayrshire
Arisaig (see Ardnamurchan)	505	Argyll
Arngask	404	Fife (also Perth & Kinross)
Arrochar	492	Dunbartonshire
Ashkirk	781	Roxburghshire
Assynt	44	Sutherland
Athelstaneford	703	E. Lothian (Haddingtonshire)
Auchindoir & Kearn	172	Aberdeenshire
Auchinleck	577	Ayrshire
Auchterarder	329	Perthshire
Auchterderran	405	Fife
Auchtergaven	330	Perthshire
Auchterhouse	273	Angus (Forfarshire)
Auchterless	173	Aberdeenshire

Local Authority	Sheriff Court	Commissary Court
Dumfries & Galloway	Dumfries SC15	Dumfries CC5
Fife	Cupar SC20	St Andrews CC20
Fife	Cupar SC20	St Andrews CC20
Dumfries & Galloway	Kirkcudbright SC16	Kirkcudbright CC13
Argyll & Bute	Dunoon SC51	Argyll CC2
Highland	Dingwall SC25	Ross CC19
Dumfries & Galloway	Dumfries SC15	Dumfries CC5
Angus	Forfar SC47	St Andrews CC20
Angus	Forfar SC47	St Andrews CC20
Aberdeenshire	Stonehaven SC5	St Andrews CC20
Argyll & Bute	Dunoon SC51	Argyll CC2
Highland	Nairn SC31	Moray CC16
Highland	Inverness SC29	Inverness CC11
Highland	Dunoon SC51	Argyll CC2
N.Ayrshire	Ayr SC6	Glasgow CC9
Highland	Dunoon SC51	Argyll CC2
Fife	Cupar SC20	Dunkeld CC7
Argyll & Bute	Dumbarton SC65	Glasgow CC9
The Scottish Borders	Jedburgh SC62	Peebles CC18
Highland	Dornoch SC9	Caithness CC4
E. Lothian	Haddington SC40	Edinburgh CC8
Aberdeenshire	Aberdeen SC1	Aberdeen CC1
E. Ayrshire	Ayr SC6	Glasgow CC9
Perthshire	Perth SC49	Dunblane CC6
Fife	Cupar SC20	St Andrews CC20
Perthshire	Perth SC49	Dunkeld CC7
Angus	Forfar SC47	Dunkeld CC7
Aberdeenshire	Aberdeen SC1	Aberdeen CC1

Parish	No.	County
Auchtermuchty	406	Fife
Auchtertool	407	Fife
Auldearn	121	Nairnshire
Avoch	59	Ross & Cromarty
Avondale	621	Lanarkshire
Ayr	578	Ayrshire
Ayton	727	Berwickshire
Baldernock	471	Stirlingshire
Balfron	472	Stirlingshire
Ballachulish & Corran of Ardgour (Q.S.)	506	Argyll
Ballantrae	579	Ayrshire
Ballingry	408	Fife
Balmaclellan	856	Kirkcudbrightshire
Balmaghie	857a	Kirkcudbrightshire
Balmerino	409	Fife
Balquhidder	331	Perthshire
Banchory Devenick	251	Kincardineshire
Banchory Ternan	252	Kincardineshire
Banff	147	Banffshire
Barony	622	Lanarkshire
Barr	580	Ayrshire
Barra	108	Inverness-shire
Barry	274	Angus (Forfarshire)
Barvas	86a	Ross & Cromarty
Bathgate	662	W. Lothian (Linlithgowshire)
Beath	410	Fife
Bedrule	782	Roxburghshire
Beith	581	Ayrshire
Belhelvie	174	Aberdeenshire

Local Authority	Sheriff Court	Commissary Court
Fife	Cupar SC20	St Andrews CC20
Fife	Cupar SC20	St Andrews CC20
Highland	Nairn SC31	Moray CC16
Highland	Dingwall SC25	Ross CC19
S. Lanarkshire	Hamilton SC37	Glasgow CC9
S. Ayrshire	Ayr SC6	Glasgow CC9
The Scottish Borders	Duns SC60	Lauder CC15
E. Dunbartonshire	Stirling SC67	Hamilton & Campsie CC10
Stirling	Stirling SC67	Glasgow CC9
Highland	Dunoon SC51	Argyll CC2
S. Ayrshire	Ayr SC6	Glasgow CC9
Fife	Cupar SC20	St Andrews CC20
Dumfries & Galloway	Kirkcudbright SC16	Kirkcudbright CC13
Dumfries & Galloway	Kirkcudbright SC16	Kirkcudbright CC13
Fife	Cupar SC20	St Andrews CC20
Stirling	Perth SC49	Dunblane CC6
Aberdeenshire	Stonehaven SC5	Aberdeen CC1
Aberdeenshire	Stonehaven SC5	Aberdeen CC1
Aberdeenshire	Banff SC2	Aberdeen CC1
City of Glasgow	Glasgow SC36	Glasgow CC9
S. Ayrshire	Ayr SC6	Glasgow CC9
Western Isles	Inverness SC29	The Isles CC12
Angus	Forfar SC47	St Andrews CC20
Western Isles	Stornoway SC33	The Isles CC12
W. Lothian	Linlithgow SC41	Edinburgh CC8
Fife	Cupar SC20	St Andrews CC20
The Scottish Borders	Jedburgh SC62	Peebles CC18
N. Ayrshire	Ayr SC6	Glasgow CC9
Aberdeenshire	Aberdeen SC1	Aberdeen CC1

Parish	No.	County
Bellie	126	Morayshire (Elginshire)
Bendochy	332	Perthshire
Benholm	253	Kincardineshire
Bervie (Inverbervie)	254	Kincardineshire
Biggar	623	Lanarkshire
Birnie	127	Morayshire (Elginshire)
Birsay	13	Orkney
Birse	175	Aberdeenshire
Blackford	333	Perthshire
Blair Atholl	334	Perthshire
Blairgowrie	335	Perthshire
Blantyre	624	Lanarkshire
Boharm	128a	Morayshire (Elginshire)
Boleskine	92	Invernessshire
Bolton	704	E. Lothian (Haddingtonshire)
Bo'ness	663	W. Lothian (Linlithgowshire)
Bonhill	493	Dunbartonshire
Borgue	858	Kirkcudbrightshire
Borthwick	674	Midlothian (Edinburghshire)
Bothkennar	473	Stirlingshire
Bothwell	625	Lanarkshire
Botriphnie	148	Banffshire
Bourtie	176	Aberdeenshire
Bowden	783	Roxburghshire
Bower	34	Caithness
Bowmore (or Kilarrow)	536	Argyll
Boyndie	149	Banffshire
Bracadale	109	Inverness-shire
Braemar (see Crathie & Braemar)	183	Aberdeenshire

Local Authority	Sheriff Court	Commissary Court
Moray	Elgin SC26	Moray CC16
Perthshire	Perth SC49	St Andrews CC20
Aberdeenshire	Stonehaven SC5	St Andrews CC20
Aberdeenshire	Stonehaven SC5	St Andrews CC20
S. Lanarkshire	Lanark SC38	Lanark CC14
Moray	Elgin SC26	Moray CC16
Orkney	Kirkwall SC11	Orkney & Shetland CC17
Aberdeenshire	Aberdeen SC1	Aberdeen CC1
Perthshire	Perth SC49	Dunblane CC6
Perthshire	Perth SC49	Dunkeld CC7
Perthshire	Perth SC49	St Andrews CC20
S. Lanarkshire	Hamilton SC37	Glasgow CC9
Moray	Banff SC2	Moray CC16
Highland	Inverness SC29	Inverness CC11
E. Lothian	Haddington SC40	Edinburgh CC8
Falkirk	Linlithgow SC41	Edinburgh CC8
West Dunbartonshire	Dumbarton SC65	Glasgow CC9
Dumfries & Galloway	Kirkcudbright SC16	Kirkcudbright CC13
Midlothian	Edinburgh SC70	Edinburgh CC8
Falkirk	Stirling SC67	Stirling CC21
N. Lanarkshire/ S. Lanarkshire	Hamilton SC37	Glasgow CC9
Moray	Banff SC2	Moray CC16
Aberdeenshire	Aberdeen SC1	Aberdeen CC1
The Scottish Borders	Jedburgh SC62	Peebles CC18
Highland	Wick SC14	Caithness CC4
Argyll and Bute	Dunoon SC51	The Isles CC12
Aberdeenshire	Banff SC2	Aberdeen CC1
Highland	Inverness SC29	The Isles CC12
Aberdeenshire	Aberdeen SC1	Aberdeen CC1

Parish	No.	County
Brechin	275	Angus (Forfarshire)
Bressay (incl Burra & Quarff)	1	Zetland
Broughton	758	Peeblesshire
Broughton (see Kilbucho)	763	Peeblesshire
Brydekirk (Q.S. From Annan)	813b	Dumfriesshire
Buchanan	474	Stirlingshire
Buittle	859	Kirkcudbrightshire
Buncle & Preston	728	Berwickshire
Burntisland	411	Fife
Burra & Quarff	1	Zetland
Burray (seeSouth Ronaldsay)	29	Orkney
Cabrach	177	Aberdeenshire (Banffshire)
Cadder	626	Lanarkshire
Caerlaverock	815	Dumfriesshire
Cairney	178	Aberdeenshire
Callander	336	Perthshire
Cambuslang	627	Lanarkshire
Cambusnethan	628	Lanarkshire
Cameron	412	Fife
Campbeltown	507	Argyll
Campsie	475	Stirlingshire
Canisbay	35	Caithness
Canonbie	814	Dumfriesshire
Caputh	337	Perthshire
Cardross	494	Dunbartonshire
Careston	277	Angus (Forfarshire)
Cargill	338	Perthshire
Carluke	629	Lanarkshire
Carmichael	630	Lanarkshire

Local Authority	Sheriff Court	Commissary Court
Angus	Forfar SC47	Brechin CC3
Shetland	Lerwick SC12	Orkney & Shetland CC17
The Scottish Borders	Peebles SC42	Peebles CC18
The Scottish Border	Peebles SC42	Peebles CC18
Dumfries & Galloway	Dumfries SC15	Dumfries CC5
Stirling	Stirling SC67	Glasgow CC9
Dumfries & Galloway	Kirkcudbright SC16	Kirkcudbright CC13
The Scottish Borders	Duns SC60	Lauder CC15
Fife	Cupar SC20	St Andrews CC20
Shetland	Lerwick SC12	Orkney & Shetland CC17
Orkney	Kirkwall SC11	Orkney & Shetland CC17
Moray	Aberdeen SC1	Aberdeen CC1
E. Dunbartonshire/ N. Lanarkshire	Glasgow SC36	Glasgow CC9
Dumfries & Galloway	Dumfries SC15	Dumfries CC5
Aberdeenshire	Aberdeen SC1	Aberdeen CC1
Stirling	Perth SC49	Dunblane CC6
S. Lanarkshire	Glasgow SC36	Glasgow CC9
N. Lanarkshire	Hamilton SC37	Glasgow CC9
Fife	Cupar SC20	St Andrews CC20
Argyll & Bute	Dunoon SC51	Argyll CC2
E. Dunbartonshire	Stirling SC67	Hamilton & Campsie CC10
Highland	Wick SC14	Caithness CC4
Dumfries & Galloway	Dumfries SC15	Dumfries CC5
Perthshire	Perth SC49	Dunkeld CC7
Argyll & Bute	Dumbarton SC65	Hamilton & Campsie CC10
Angus	Forfar SC47	Brechin CC3
Perthshire	Perth SC49	Dunkeld CC7
S. Lanarkshire	Lanark SC38	Lanark CC14
S. Lanarkshire	Hamilton SC37	Lanark CC14

Parish	No.	County
Carmunnock	631	Lanarkshire
Carmyllie	276	Angus (Forfarshire)
Carnbee	413	Fife
Carnock	414	Fife
Carnwath	632	Lanarkshire
Carriden	664	W. Lothian (Linlithgowshire)
Carrington	675	Midlothian (Edinburghshire)
Carsphairn	860	Kirkcudbrightshire
Carstairs	633	Lanarkshire
Castleton	784	Roxburghshire
Cathcart	560	Renfrewshire
Cavers	785	Roxburghshire
Cawdor	122	Nairnshire
Ceres	415	Fife
Channelkirk	729	Berwickshire
Chapel of Garioch	179	Aberdeenshire
Chirnside	730	Berwickshire
Clackmannan	466	Clackmannanshire
Clatt	180	Aberdeenshire
Cleish	460	Kinross
Closeburn	816	Dumfriesshire
Clunie	339	Perthshire
Cluny	181	Aberdeenshire
Clyne	45	Sutherland
Cockburnspath	731	Berwickshire
Cockpen	676	Midlothian (Edinburghshire)
Coldingham	732	Berwickshire
Coldstream (formerly Lennel)	733	Berwickshire
Colinton (or Hailes)	677	Midlothian (Edinburghshire)
Coll (see Tiree)	551	Argyll

Local Authority	Sheriff Court	Commissary Court
S. Lanarkshire	Glasgow SC36	Glasgow CC9
Angus	Forfar SC47	Brechin CC3
Fife	Cupar SC20	St Andrews CC20
Fife	Cupar SC20	Stirling CC21
S. Lanarkshire	Lanark SC38	Lanark CC14
Falkirk	Linlithgow SC41	Edinburgh CC8
Midlothian	Edinburgh SC70	Edinburgh CC8
Dumfries & Galloway	Kirkcudbright SC16	Kirkcudbright CC13
S. Lanarkshire	Lanark SC38	Lanark CC14
The Scottish Borders	Jedburgh SC62	Peebles CC18
E. Renfrewshire/Glasgow	Paisley SC58	Glasgow CC9
The Scottish Borders	Jedburgh SC62	Peebles CC18
Highland	Nairn SC31	Moray CC16
Fife	Cupar SC20	St Andrews CC20
The Scottish Borders	Duns SC60	Lauder CC15
Aberdeenshire	Aberdeen SC1	Aberdeen CC1
The Scottish Borders	Duns SC60	Lauder CC15
Clackmannan	Alloa SC64	Stirling CC21
Aberdeenshire	Aberdeen SC1	Aberdeen CC1
Perthshire	Kinross SC22	St Andrews CC20
Dumfries & Galloway	Dumfries SC15	Dumfries CC5
Perthshire	Perth SC49	Dunkeld CC7
Aberdeenshire	Aberdeen SC1	Aberdeen CC1
Highland	Dornoch SC9	Caithness CC4
The Scottish Borders	Duns SC60	Lauder CC15
Midlothian	Edinburgh SC70	Edinburgh CC8
The Scottish Borders	Duns SC60	Lauder CC15
The Scottish Borders	Duns SC60	Lauder CC15
City of Edinburgh	Edinburgh SC70	Edinburgh CC8
Argyll & Bute	Dunoon SC51	The Isles CC12

Parish	No.	County
Collace	340	Perthshire
Collessie	416	Fife
Colmonell	582	Ayrshire
Colonsay (see Jura)	539	Argyll
Colvend & Southwick	861	Kirkcudbrightshire
Comrie	341	Perthshire
Contin	60	Ross & Cromarty
Corstorphine	678	Midlothian (Edinburghshire)
Cortachy & Clova	278	Angus (Forfarshire)
Coull	182	Aberdeenshire
Coupar-Angus	279	Perthshire/Angus (Forfarshire)
Covington & Thankerton	634	Lanarkshire
Coylton	583	Ayrshire
Craig (Inchbrayock)	280	Angus (Forfarshire)
Craigie	584	Ayrshire
Craignish	508	Argyll
Crail	417	Fife
Crailing	786	Roxburghshire
Cramond	679	Midlothian (Edinburghshire)
Cranshaws	734	Berwickshire
Cranston	680	Midlothian (Edinburghshire)
Crathie & Braemar	183	Aberdeenshire
Crawford (incl Leadhills)	635	Lanarkshire
Crawfordjohn	636	Lanarkshire
Creich	46	Sutherland
Creich	418	Fife
Crichton	681	Midlothian (Edinburghshire)
Crieff	342	Perthshire
Crimond	184	Aberdeenshire

Local Authority	Sheriff Court	Commissary Court
Perthshire	Perth SC49	St Andrews CC20
Fife	Cupar SC20	St Andrews CC20
S. Ayrshire	Ayr SC6	Glasgow CC9
Argyll & Bute	Dunoon SC51	The Isles CC12
Dumfries & Galloway	Kirkcudbright SC16	Dumfries CC5
Perthshire	Perth SC49	Dunblane CC6
Highland	Dingwall SC25	Ross CC19
City of Edinburgh	Edinburgh SC70	Edinburgh CC8
Angus	Forfar SC47	Brechin CC3
Aberdeenshire	Aberdeen SC1	Aberdeen CC1
Perthshire	Forfar SC47	Dunkeld CC7
S. Lanarkshire	Lanark SC38	Lanark CC14
E. Ayrshire	Ayr SC6	Glasgow CC9
Angus	Forfar SC47	St Andrews CC20
S. Ayrshire	Ayr SC6	Glasgow CC9
Argyll & Bute	Dunoon SC51	Argyll CC2
Fife	Cupar SC20	St Andrews CC20
The Scottish Borders	Jedburgh SC62	Peebles CC18
City of Edinburgh	Edinburgh SC70	Edinburgh CC8
The Scottish Borders	Duns SC60	Lauder CC15
Midlothian	Edinburgh SC70	Edinburgh CC8
Aberdeenshire	Aberdeen SC1	Aberdeen CC1
S. Lanarkshire	Lanark SC38	Lanark CC14
S. Lanarkshire	Lanark SC38	Lanark CC14
Highland	Dornoch SC9	Caithness CC4
Fife	Cupar SC20	St Andrews CC20
Midlothian	Edinburgh SC70	Edinburgh CC8
Perthshire	Perth SC49	Dunkeld CC7
Aberdeenshire	Aberdeen SC1	Aberdeen CC1

Parish	No.	County
Cromarty	61	Ross & Cromarty
Cromdale (incl Inverallan & Advie)	128b	Morayshire (Elginshire)
Crossmichael	863	Kirkcudbrightshire
Croy & Dalcross	94	Invernessshire
Cruden	185	Aberdeenshire
Cullen	150	Banffshire
Culross	343	Perthshire (later Fife)
Culsalmond	186	Aberdeenshire
Culter	637	Lanarkshire
Cults	419	Fife
Cumbernauld	495	Dunbartonshire
Cumbraes	552	Buteshire
Cummertrees	817	Dumfriesshire
Cunningsburgh (see Dunrossness)	2	Zetland
Cupar	420	Fife
Currie	682	Midlothian (Edinburghshire)
Dailly	585	Ayrshire
Dairsie	421	Fife
Dalavich (see Kilchrenan & Dalavich)	517	Argyll
Dalcross (see Croy & Dalcross)	94	Inverness-shire
Dalgety	422	Fife
Dalkeith	683	Midlothian (Edinburghshire)
Dallas	129	Morayshire (Elginshire)
Dalmellington	586	Ayrshire
Dalmeny	665	W. Lothian (Linlithgowshire)
Dalry	587	Ayrshire
Dalry	865	Kirkcudbrightshire
Dalrymple	588	Ayrshire

Local Authority	Sheriff Court	Commissary Court
Highland	Dingwall SC25	Ross CC19
Highland	Elgin SC26	Moray CC16
Dumfries & Galloway	Kirkcudbright SC16	Kirkcudbright CC13
Highland	Inverness SC29	Inverness CC11
Aberdeenshire	Aberdeen SC1	Aberdeen CC1
Moray	Banff SC2	Aberdeen CC1
Fife	Perth SC49	Dunblane CC6
Aberdeenshire	Aberdeen SC1	Aberdeen CC1
S. Lanarkshire	Lanark SC38	Lanark CC14
Fife	Cupar SC20	St Andrews CC20
N. Lanarkshire	Dumbarton SC65	Glasgow CC9
N. Ayrshire	Rothesay SC8	The Isles CC12
Dumfries & Galloway	Dumfries SC15	Dumfries CC5
Shetland	Lerwick SC12	Orkney & Shetland CC17
Fife	Cupar SC20	St Andrews CC20
City of Edinburgh	Edinburgh SC70	Edinburgh CC8
S. Ayrshire	Ayr SC6	Glasgow CC9
Fife	Cupar SC20	St Andrews CC20
Argyll & Bute	Dunoon SC51	Argyll CC2
Highland	Inverness SC29	Inverness CC11
Fife	Cupar SC20	St Andrews CC20
Midlothian	Edinburgh SC70	Edinburgh CC8
Moray	Elgin SC26	Moray CC16
E. Ayrshire	Ayr SC6	Glasgow CC9
City of Edinburgh	Linlithgow SC41	Edinburgh CC8
N. Ayrshire	Ayr SC6	Glasgow CC9
Dumfries & Galloway	Kirkcudbright SC16	Kirkcudbright CC13
E. Ayrshire	Ayr SC6	Glasgow CC9

Parish	No.	County
Dalserf	638	Lanarkshire
Dalton	818	Dumfriesshire
Dalziel	639	Lanarkshire
Daviot	187	Aberdeenshire
Daviot & Dunlichty	95	Invernessshire
Deerness	14	Orkney
Delting	2	Zetland
Denny	476	Stirlingshire
Deskford	151	Banffshire
Dingwall	62	Ross & Cromarty
Dirleton	705	E. Lothian (Haddingtonshire)
Dollar	467	Clackmannanshire
Dolphinton	640	Lanarkshire
Dores	96a	Invernessshire
Dornoch	47	Sutherland
Dornock	819	Dumfriesshire
Douglas	641	Lanarkshire
Dowally	344	Perthshire
Drainie (Kinneddar)	130	Morayshire (Elginshire)
Dreghorn	589	Ayrshire
Dron	345	Perthshire
Drumblade	188	Aberdeenshire
Drumelzier	759	Peeblesshire
Drumoak	189	Aberdeenshire
Dryfesdale	820	Dumfriesshire
Drymen	477	Stirlingshire
Duddingston	684	Midlothian (Edinburghshire)
Duffus	131	Morayshire (Elginshire)
Duirinish	110	Invernessshire
Dull	346	Perthshire

Local Authority	Sheriff Court	Commissary Court
S. Lanarkshire	Hamilton SC37	Hamilton & Campsie CC10
Dumfries & Galloway	Dumfries SC15	Dumfries CC5
N. Lanarkshire	Hamilton SC37	Glasgow CC9
Aberdeenshire	Aberdeen SC1	Aberdeen CC1
Highland	Inverness SC29	Inverness CC11
Orkney	Kirkwall SC11	Orkney & Shetland CC17
Shetland	Lerwick SC12	Orkney & Shetland CC17
Falkirk	Stirling SC67	Stirling CC21
Moray	Banff SC2	Aberdeen CC1
Highland	Dingwall SC25	Ross CC19
E. Lothian	Haddington SC40	Edinburgh CC8
Clackmannan	Alloa SC64	Stirling CC21
S. Lanarkshire	Lanark SC38	Lanark CC14
Highland	Inverness SC29	Inverness C11
Highland	Dornoch SC9	Caithness CC4
Dumfries & Galloway	Dumfries SC15	Dumfries CC5
S. Lanarkshire	Lanark SC38	Lanark CC14
Perthshire	Perth SC49	Dunkeld CC7
Moray	Elgin SC26	Moray CC16
N. Ayrshire	Ayr SC6	Glasgow CC9
Perthshire	Perth SC49	Dunblane CC6
Aberdeenshire	Aberdeen SC1	Aberdeen CC1
The Scottish Borders	Peebles SC42	Peebles CC18
Aberdeenshire	Aberdeen SC1	Aberdeen CC1
Dumfries & Galloway	Dumfries SC15	Dumfries CC5
Stirling	Stirling SC67	Glasgow CC9
City of Edinburgh	Edinburgh SC70	Edinburgh CC8
Moray	Elgin SC26	Moray CC16
Highland	Inverness SC29	The Isles CC12
Perthshire	Perth SC49	Dunkeld CC7

Parish	No.	County
Dumbarton	496	Dunbartonshire
Dumfries	821	Dumfriesshire
Dun	281	Angus (Forfarshire)
Dunbar	706	E. Lothian (Haddingtonshire)
Dunbarney	347	Perthshire
Dunblane	348	Perthshire
Dunbog	423	Fife
Dundee	282	Angus (Forfarshire)
Dundonald	590	Ayrshire
Dundurcas (see Rothes)	141	Morayshire (Elginshire)
Dunfermline	424	Fife
Dunino	425	Fife
Dunipace	478	Stirlingshire
Dunkeld	349	Perthshire
Dunlichty (see Daviot & Dunlichty)	95	Invernessshire
Dunlop	591	Ayrshire
Dunnet	36	Caithness
Dunnichen	283	Angus (Forfarshire)
Dunning	350	Perthshire
Dunnottar	255	Kincardineshire
Dunoon & Kilmun	510	Argyll
Dunrossness (inc. Sandwick, Cunningsburgh)	3	Zetland
Duns	735	Berwickshire
Dunscore	822	Dumfriesshire
Dunsyre	642	Lanarkshire
Durness	48	Sutherland
Durris	256	Kincardineshire
Durrisdeer	823	Dumfriesshire

Local Authority	Sheriff Court	Commissary Court
W. Dunbartonshire	Dumbarton SC65	Glasgow CC9
Dumfries & Galloway	Dumfries SC15	Dumfries CC5
Angus	Forfar SC47	St Andrews CC20
E. Lothian	Haddington SC40	Edinburgh CC8
Perthshire	Perth SC49	St Andrews CC20
Stirling	Perth SC49	Dunblane CC6
Fife	Cupar SC20	St Andrews CC20
Dundee	Dundee SC45	Brechin CC3
S. Ayrshire	Ayr SC6	Glasgow CC9
Moray	Elgin SC26	Moray CC16
Fife	Cupar SC20	St Andrews CC20
Fife	Cupar SC20	St Andrews CC20
Falkirk	Stirling SC67	Stirling CC21
Perthshire	Perth SC49	Dunkeld CC7
Highland	Inverness SC29	Inverness CC11
E. Ayrshire	Ayr SC6	Glasgow CC9
Highland	Wick SC14	Caithness CC4
Angus	Forfar SC47	Brechin CC3
Perthshire	Perth SC49	Dunblane CC6
Aberdeenshire	Stonehaven SC5	St Andrews CC20
Argyll and Bute	Dunoon SC51	Argyll CC2
Shetland	Lerwick SC12	Orkney & Shetland CC17
The Scottish Borders	Duns SC60	Lauder CC15
Dumfries & Galloway	Dumfries SC15	Dumfries CC5
S. Lanarkshire	Lanark SC38	Lanark CC14
Highland	Dornoch SC9	Caithness CC4
Aberdeenshire	Stonehaven SC5	St Andrews CC20
Dumfries & Galloway	Dumfries SC15	Dumfries CC5

Parish	No.	County
Duthil & Rothiemurcus	96b	Invernessshire
Dyce	190	Aberdeenshire
Dyke	133	Morayshire (Elginshire)
Dysart	426	Fife
Eaglesham	561	Renfrewshire
Earlston	736	Berwickshire
Eassie & Nevay	284	Angus (Forfarshire)
East Calder (see Kirknewton)	690	Midlothian (Edinburghshire)
East Kilbride	643	Lanarkshire
Eastwood	562	Renfrewshire
Eccles	737	Berwickshire
Ecclesmachan	666	W. Lothian (Linlithgowshire)
Echt	191	Aberdeenshire
Eckford	787a	Roxburghshire
Eday & Pharay	15	Orkney
Edderton	63	Ross & Cromarty
Eddlestone	760	Peeblesshire
Eddrachillis	49	Sutherland
Edinburgh	685-1	Midlothian (Edinburghshire)
Edinburgh – Canongate	685-3	Midlothian (Edinburghshire)
Edinburgh – St Cuthbert's	685-2	Midlothian (Edinburghshire)
Edinkillie	134	Morayshire (Elginshire)
Ednam	788	Roxburghshire
Edrom	738	Berwickshire
Edzell	285	Angus (Forfarshire)
Elgin	135	Morayshire (Elginshire)
Elie	427	Fife
Ellon	192	Aberdeenshire
Enzie	152	Banffshire
Errol	351	Perthshire

Local Authority	Sheriff Court	Commissary Court
Highland	Inverness SC29	Inverness CC11
Aberdeen City	Aberdeen SC1	Aberdeen CC1
Moray	Elgin SC26	Moray CC16
Fife	Cupar SC20	St Andrews CC20
E. Renfrewshire	Paisley SC58	Glasgow CC9
The Scottish Borders	Duns SC60	Lauder CC15
Angus	Forfar SC47	St Andrews CC20
W. Lothian	Edinburgh SC70	Edinburgh CC8
S. Lanarkshire	Hamilton SC37	Hamilton & Campsie CC10
E. Renfrewshire	Paisley SC58	Glasgow CC9
The Scottish Borders	Duns SC60	Lauder CC15
W. Lothian	Linlithgow SC41	Edinburgh CC8
Aberdeenshire	Aberdeen SC1	Aberdeen CC1
The Scottish Borders	Jedburgh SC62	Peebles CC18
Orkney	Kirkwall SC11	Orkney & Shetland CC17
Highland	Dingwall SC25	Ross CC19
The Scottish Borders	Peebles SC42	Peebles CC18
Highland	Dornoch SC9	Caithness CC4
City of Edinburgh	Edinburgh SC70	Edinburgh CC8
City of Edinburgh	Edinburgh SC70	Edinburgh CC8
City of Edinburgh	Edinburgh SC70	Edinburgh CC8
Moray	Elgin SC26	Moray CC16
The Scottish Borders	Jedburgh SC62	Peebles CC18
The Scottish Borders	Duns SC60	Lauder CC15
Angus	Forfar SC47	St Andrews CC20
Moray	Elgin SC26	Moray CC16
Fife	Cupar SC20	St Andrews CC20
Aberdeenshire	Aberdeen SC1	Aberdeen CC1
Moray	Banff SC2	Moray CC16
Perthshire	Perth SC49	St Andrews CC20

Parish	No.	County
Erskine	563	Renfrewshire
Eskdalemuir	824	Dumfriesshire
Essil & Dipple (Speymouth)	143	Morayshire (Elginshire)
Ettrick	774b	Selkirkshire
Evie & Rendall	16	Orkney
Ewes	825	Dumfriesshire
Eyemouth	739	Berwickshire
Fala & Soutra	686	Midlothian (Edinburghshire)
Falkirk	479	Stirlingshire
Falkland	428	Fife
Farnell	286	Angus (Forfarshire)
Farr	50	Sutherland
Fearn	64	Ross & Cromarty
Fearn	287	Angus (Forfarshire)
Fenwick	592	Ayrshire
Ferry Port On Craig	429	Fife
Fetlar (incl North Yell)	4	Zetland
Fettercairn	257	Kincardineshire
Fetteresso	258	Kincardineshire
Findo-Gask	352	Perthshire
Fintray	193	Aberdeenshire
Fintry	480	Stirlingshire
Firth & Stenness	17	Orkney
Flisk	430	Fife
Flotta (See Walls)	32	Orkney
Fodderty	65	Ross & Cromarty
Fogo	740	Berwickshire
Fordoun	259	Kincardineshire
Fordyce	153	Banffshire
Forfar	288	Angus (Forfarshire)

Local Authority	Sheriff Court	Commissary Court
Renfrewshire	Paisley SC58	Glasgow CC9
Dumfries & Galloway	Dumfries SC15	Dumfries CC5
Moray	Elgin SC26	Moray CC16
The Scottish Borders	Selkirk SC63	Peebles CC18
Orkney	Kirkwall SC11	Orkney & Shetland CC17
Dumfries & Galloway	Dumfries SC15	Dumfries CC5
The Scottish Borders	Duns SC60	Lauder CC15
Midlothian	Edinburgh SC70	Edinburgh CC8
Falkirk	Stirling SC67	Stirling CC21
Fife	Cupar SC20	St Andrews CC20
Angus	Forfar SC47	Brechin CC3
Highland	Dornoch SC9	Caithness CC4
Highland	Dingwall SC25	Ross CC19
Angus	Forfar SC47	Brechin CC3
E. Ayrshire	Ayr SC6	Glasgow CC9
Fife	Cupar SC20	St Andrews CC20
Shetland	Lerwick SC12	Orkney & Shetland CC17
Aberdeenshire	Stonehaven SC5	St Andrews CC20
Aberdeenshire	Stonehaven SC5	St Andrews CC20
Perthshire	Perth SC49	Dunblane CC6
Aberdeenshire	Aberdeen SC1	Aberdeen CC1
Stirling	Stirling SC67	Glasgow CC9
Orkney	Kirkwall SC11	Orkney & Shetland CC17
Fife	Cupar SC20	St Andrews CC20
Orkney	Kirkwall SC11	Orkney & ShetlandCC17
Highland	Dingwall SC25	Ross CC19
The Scottish Borders	Duns SC60	Lauder CC15
Aberdeenshire	Stonehaven SC5	St Andrews CC20
Aberdeenshire	Banff SC2	Aberdeen CC1
Angus	Forfar SC47	St Andrews CC20

Parish	No.	County
Forgan	431	Fife
Forgandenny	353	Perthshire
Forglen	154	Banffshire
Forgue	194	Aberdeenshire
Forres	137	Morayshire (Elginshire)
Forteviot	354	Perthshire
Fortingall	355a	Perthshire
Fossoway & Tulliebole	461	Kinrosssshire
Foula (See Walls)	12	Zetland
Foulden	741	Berwickshire
Foveran	195	Aberdeenshire
Fowlis Easter	356	Perthshire (later Angus)
Fowlis Wester	357	Perthshire
Fraserburgh	196	Aberdeenshire
Fyvie	197	Aberdeenshire
Gairloch	66	Ross & Cromarty
Galashiels	775	Selkirkshire
Galston	593	Ayrshire
Gamrie (incl Macduff & Down)	155a	Banffshire
Gargunnock	481	Stirlingshire
Gartly	198	Aberdeenshire
Garvald & Bara	707	E. Lothian (Haddingtonshire)
Garvock	260	Kincardineshire
Gigha & Cara	537	Argyll
Girthon	866	Kirkcudbrightshire
Girvan	594	Ayrshire
Gladsmuir	708	E. Lothian (Haddingtonshire)
Glamis	289	Angus (Forfarshire)
Glasgow	644-1	Lanarkshire
Glass	199	Aberdeenshire

Local Authority	Sheriff Court	Commissary Court
Fife	Cupar SC20	St Andrews CC20
Perthshire	Perth SC49	Dunkeld CC7
Aberdeenshire	Banff SC2	Aberdeen CC1
Aberdeenshire	Aberdeen SC1	Aberdeen CC1
Moray	Elgin SC26	Moray CC16
Perthshire	Perth SC49	St Andrews CC20
Perthshire	Perth SC49	Dunkeld CC7
Perthshire	Kinross SC22	St Andrews CC20
Shetland	Lerwick SC12	Orkney & Shetland CC17
The Scottish Borders	Duns SC60	Lauder CC15
Aberdeenshire	Aberdeen SC1	Aberdeen CC1
Angus	Forfar SC47	St Andrews CC20
Perthshire	Perth SC49	Dunblane CC6
Aberdeenshire	Aberdeen SC1	Aberdeen CC1
Aberdeenshire	Aberdeen SC1	Aberdeen CC1
Highland	Dingwall SC25	Ross CC19
The Scottish Borders	Selkirk SC63	Peebles CC18
East Ayrshire	Ayr SC6	Glasgow CC9
Aberdeenshire	Banff SC2	Aberdeen CC1
Stirling	Stirling SC67	Stirling CC21
Aberdeenshire	Aberdeen SC1	Moray CC16
E. Lothian	Haddington SC40	Edinburgh CC8
Aberdeenshire	Stonehaven SC5	St Andrews CC20
Argyll & Bute	Dunoon SC51	The Isles CC12
Dumfries & Galloway	Kirkcudbright SC16	Kirkcudbright CC13
S. Ayrshire	Ayr SC6	Glasgow CC9
E. Lothian	Haddington SC40	Edinburgh CC8
Angus	Forfar SC47	St Andrews CC20
City of Glasgow	Glasgow SC36	Glasgow CC9
Aberdeenshire	Aberdeen SC1	Moray CC16

Parish	No.	County
Glassary	511	Argyll
Glasserton	885	Wigtownshire
Glassford	645	Lanarkshire
Glenbervie	261	Kincardineshire
Glenbuchat (Glenbucket)	200	Aberdeenshire
Glencairn	826	Dumfriesshire
Glencorse (formerly Woodhouselee)	687	Midlothian (Edinburghshire)
Glendevon	358	Perthshire
Glenelg	97	Inverness-shire
Glenholm	761	Peeblesshire
Glenisla	290	Angus (Forfarshire)
Glenluce (see Old Luce)	894	Wigtownshire
Glenmoriston (see Urquhart)	107	Inverness-shire
Glenmuck, Tullich & Glengairn	201	Aberdeenshire
Glenorchy & Inishail	512	Argyll
Glenshiel	67	Ross & Cromarty
Golspie	51	Sutherland
Gorbals	644-2	Lanarkshire
Gordon	742	Berwickshire
Govan	646	Lanarkshire
Graemsay (see Hoy)	20	Orkney
Grange	156	Banffshire
Greenlaw	743	Berwickshire
Greenock (Middle, East & West)	564	Renfrewshire
Gretna (Graitney)	827	Dumfriesshire
Guthrie	291	Angus (Forfarshire)
Haddington	709	E. Lothian (Haddingtonshire)
Halfmorton	828	Dumfriesshire
Halkirk	37	Caithness

Local Authority	Sheriff Court	Commissary Court
Argyll & Bute	Dunoon SC51	Argyll CC2
Dumfries & Galloway	Wigtown SC19	Wigtown CC22
S. Lanarkshire	Hamilton SC37	Hamilton & Campsie CC10
Aberdeenshire	Stonehaven SC5	Brechin CC3
Aberdeenshire	Aberdeen SC1	Aberdeen CC1
Dumfries & Galloway	Dumfries SC15	Dumfries CC5
Midlothian	Edinburgh SC70	Edinburgh CC8
Perthshire	Perth SC49	Dunblane CC6
Highland	Inverness SC29	Argyll CC2
The Scottish Borders	Peebles SC42	Peebles CC18
Angus	Forfar SC47	Brechin CC3
Dumfries & Galloway	Wigtown SC19	Wigtown CC22
Highland	Inverness SC29	Inverness CC11
Aberdeenshire	Aberdeen SC1	Aberdeen CC1
Argyll and Bute	Dunoon SC51	Argyll CC2
Highland	Dingwall SC25	Ross CC19
Highland	Dornoch SC9	Caithness CC4
City of Glasgow	Glasgow SC36	Hamilton & Campsie CC10
The Scottish Borders	Duns SC60	Lauder CC15
City of Glasgow	Glasgow SC36	Hamilton & Campsie CC10
Orkney	Kirkwall SC11	Orkney & Shetland CC17
Moray	Banff SC2	Moray CC16
The Scottish Borders	Duns SC60	Lauder CC15
Inverclyde	Paisley SC58	Glasgow CC9
Dumfries and Galloway	Dumfries SC15	Dumfries CC5
Angus	Forfar SC47	Brechin CC3
E. Lothian	Haddington SC40	Edinburgh CC8
Dumfries & Galloway	Dumfries SC15	Dumfries CC5
Highland	Wick SC14	Caithness CC4

Parish	No.	County
Hamilton	647	Lanarkshire
Harray	18	Orkney
Harris (incl. St Kilda)	111	Inverness-shire
Hawick	789	Roxburghshire
Heriot	688	Midlothian (Edinburghshire)
Hobkirk	790	Roxburghshire
Hoddam	829	Dumfriesshire
Holm & Paplay	19	Orkney
Holywood	830	Dumfriesshire
Houston & Killellan	565	Renfrewshire
Hownam	791	Roxburghshire
Hoy & Graemsay	20	Orkney
Humbie	710	E.Lothian (Haddingtonshire)
Huntly	202	Aberdeenshire
Hutton	745	Berwickshire
Hutton & Corrie	831	Dumfriesshire
Inch	886	Wigtownshire
Inchinnan	566	Renfrewshire
Inchture	359	Perthshire
Inishail (see Glenorchy & Inishail)	512	Argll
Innerleithen	762	Peeblesshire
Innerwick	711	E. Lothian (Haddingtonshire)
Insch	203	Aberdeenshire
Inveraray & Glenaray	513	Argyll
Inverarity & Methy	292	Angus (Forfarshire)
Inveravon	157	Banffshire
Inverbervie (see Bervie)	254	Kincardineshire
Inveresk	689	Midlothian (Edinburghshire)
Inverkeillor	293	Angus (Forfarshire)
Inverkeithing	432	Fife

Local Authority	Sheriff Court	Commissary Court
S. Lanarkshire	Hamilton SC37	Hamilton & Campsie CC10
Orkney	Kirkwall SC11	Orkney & Shetland CC17
Western Isles	Inverness SC29	The Isles CC12
The Scottish Borders	Jedburgh SC62	Peebles CC18
The Scottish Borders	Edinburgh SC70	Edinburgh CC8
The Scottish Borders	Jedburgh SC62	Peebles CC18
Dumfries & Galloway	Dumfries SC15	Dumfries CC5
Orkney	Kirkwall SC11	Orkney & Shetland CC17
Dumfries and Galloway	Dumfries SC15	Dumfries CC5
Renfrewshire	Paisley SC58	Glasgow CC9
The Scottish Borders	Jedburgh SC62	Peebles CC18
Orkney	Kirkwall SC11	Orkney & Shetland CC17
E.Lothian	Haddington SC40	Edinburgh CC8
Aberdeenshire	Aberdeen SC1	Aberdeen CC1
The Scottish Borders	Duns SC60	Lauder CC15
Dumfries and Galloway	Dumfries SC15	Dumfries CC5
Dumfries and Galloway	Wigtown SC19	Wigtown CC22
Renfrewshire	Paisley SC58	Glasgow CC9
Perthshire	Perth SC49	St Andrews CC20
Argyll & Bute	Dunoon SC51	Argyll CC2
The Scottish Borders	Peebles SC42	Peebles CC18
E. Lothian	Haddington SC40	Edinburgh CC8
Aberdeenshire	Aberdeen SC1	Aberdeen CC1
Argyll and Bute	Dunoon SC51	Argyll CC2
Angus	Forfar SC47	St Andrews CC20
Moray	Banff SC2	Moray CC16
Aberdeenshire	Stonehaven SC5	St Andrews CC20
E. Lothian	Edinburgh SC70	Edinburgh CC8
Angus	Forfar SC47	St Andrews CC20
Fife	Cupar SC20	St Andrews CC20

Parish	No.	County
Inverkeithny	158	Banffshire
Inverkip	567	Renfrewshire
Inverness	98	Invernessshire
Inverurie	204	Aberdeenshire
Iona	538	Argyll
Irongray (Kirkpatrick-Irongray)	867	Kirkcudbrightshire
Irvine	595	Ayrshire
Jedburgh	792	Roxburghshire
Johnstone	832	Dumfriesshire
Jura & Colonsay	539	Argyll
Keig	205	Aberdeenshire
Keir	833	Dumfriesshire
Keith	159	Banffshire
Keithhall & Kinkell	206	Aberdeenshire
Kells	868	Kirkcudbrightshire
Kelso	793	Roxburghshire
Kelton	869	Kircudbrightshire
Kemback	433	Fife
Kemnay	207	Aberdeenshire
Kenmore	360	Perthshire
Kennethmont	212	Aberdeenshire
Kennoway	434	Fife
Kettins	294	Angus (Forfarshire)
Kettle	435	Fife
Kilarrow (see Bowmore)	536	Argyll
Kilbarchan	568	Renfrewshire
Kilberry	516	Argyll
(see Kilcalmonell & Kilberry)		
Kilbirnie	596	Ayrshire
Kilbrandon & Kilchattan	515	Argyll

Local Authority	Sheriff Court	Commissary Court
Aberdeenshire	Banff SC2	Moray CC16
Inverclyde	Paisley SC58	Glasgow CC9
Highland	Inverness SC29	Inverness CC11
Aberdeenshire	Aberdeen SC1	Aberdeen CC1
Argyll & Bute	Dunoon SC51	The Isles CC12
Dumfries & Galloway	Kirkcudbright SC16	Dumfries CC5
N. Ayrshire	Ayr SC6	Glasgow CC9
The Scottish Borders	Jedburgh SC62	Peebles CC18
Dumfries & Galloway	Dumfries SC15	Dumfries CC5
Argyll & Bute	Dunoon SC51	The Isles CC12
Aberdeenshire	Aberdeen SC1	Aberdeen CC1
Dumfries & Galloway	Dumfries SC15	Dumfries CC5
Moray	Banff SC2	Moray CC16
Aberdeenshire	Aberdeen SC1	Aberdeen CC1
Dumfries & Galloway	Kirkcudbright SC16	Kirkcudbright CC13
The Scottish Borders	Jedburgh SC62	Peebles CC18
Dumfries & Galloway	Kirkcudbright SC16	Kirkcudbright CC13
Fife	Cupar SC20	St Andrews CC20
Aberdeenshire	Aberdeen SC1	Aberdeen CC1
Perthshire	Perth SC49	Dunkeld CC7
Aberdeenshire	Aberdeen SC1	Aberdeen CC1
Fife	Cupar SC20	St Andrews CC20
Perthshire	Forfar SC47	St Andrews CC20
Fife	Cupar SC20	St Andrews CC20
Argyll & Bute	Dunoon SC51	The Isles CC12
Renfrewshire	Paisley SC58	Glasgow CC9
Argyll & Bute	Dunoon SC51	Argyll CC2
N. Ayrshire	Ayr SC6	Glasgow CC9
Argyll & Bute	Dunoon SC51	Argyll CC2

Parish	No.	County
Kilbride (Bute)	553	Buteshire
Kilbucho, Broughton & Glenholm	763	Peeblesshire
Kilcalmonell & Kilberry	516	Argyll
Kilchoman	540	Argyll
Kilchrenan & Dalavich	517	Argyll
Kilconquhar	436	Fife
Kildalton	541	Argyll
Kildonan	52	Sutherland
Kildrummy	208	Aberdeenshire
Kilfinan	518	Argyll
Kilfinichan & Kilvickeon	542	Argyll
Killean & Kilchenzie	519	Argyll
Killearn	482	Stirlingshire
Killearnan	68	Ross & Cromarty
Killellan (see Houston)	565	Renfrewshire
Killin	361	Perthshire
Kilmacolm	569	Renfrewshire
Kilmadock	362	Perthshire
Kilmallie	520	Argyll/Inverness-shire
Kilmany	437	Fife
Kilmarnock	597	Ayrshire
Kilmaronock	497	Dunbartonshire
Kilmartin	521	Argyll
Kilmaurs	598	Ayrshire
Kilmodan (Glendaruel)	522	Argyll
Kilmonivaig	99	Inverness-shire
Kilmorack	100	Inverness-shire
Kilmore & Kilbride	523	Argyll
Kilmore (Mull) (see Kilninian & Kilmore)	544	Argyll

Local Authority	Sheriff Court	Commissary Court
N. Ayrshire	Rothesay SC8	The Isles CC12
The Scottish Borders	Peebles SC42	Peebles CC18
Argyll & Bute	Dunoon SC51	Argyll CC2
Argyll & Bute	Dunoon SC51	The Isles CC12
Argyll & Bute	Dunoon SC51	Argyll CC2
Fife	Cupar SC20	St Andrews CC20
Argyll & Bute	Dunoon SC51	The Isles CC12
Highland	Dornoch SC9	Caithness CC4
Aberdeenshire	Aberdeen SC1	Aberdeen CC1
Argyll & Bute	Dunoon SC51	Argyll CC2
Argyll & Bute	Dunoon SC51	The Isles CC12
Argyll & Bute	Dunoon SC51	Argyll CC2
Stirling	Stirling SC67	Glasgow CC9
Highland	Dingwall SC25	Ross CC19
Renfrewshire	Paisley SC58	Glasgow CC9
Stirling	Perth SC49	Dunkeld CC7
Inverclyde	Paisley SC58	Glasgow CC9
Stirling	Perth SC49	Dunblane CC6
Highland	Dunoon SC51	Argyll CC2
Fife	Cupar SC20	St Andrews CC20
E. Ayrshire	Ayr SC6	Glasgow CC9
W. Dunbartonshire	Dumbarton SC65	Glasgow CC9
Argyll & Bute	Dunoon SC51	Argyll CC2
E. Ayrshire	Ayr SC6	Glasgow CC9
Argyll & Bute	Dunoon SC51	Argyll CC2
Highland	Inverness SC29	Argyll CC2
Highland	Inverness SC29	Inverness CC11
Argyll & Bute	Dunoon SC51	Argyll CC2
Argyll & Bute	Dunoon SC51	The Isles CC12

Parish	No.	County
Kilmorich (see Lochgoilhead & Kilmorich)	527	Argyll
Kilmory	554	Buteshire
Kilmuir	112	Invernessshire
Kilmuir Easter	69	Ross & Cromarty
Kilmun (see Dunoon & Kilmun)	510	Argyll
Kilninian & Kilmore	544	Argyll
Kilninver & Kilmelfort	524	Argyll
Kilrenny	438	Fife
Kilspindie	363	Perthshire
Kilsyth (formerly Monyabroch)	483	Stirlingshire
Kiltarlity	101	Inverness-shire
Kiltearn	70	Ross & Cromarty
Kilwinning	599	Ayrshire
Kincardine (Perthshire)	364	Perthshire
Kincardine (Inverness) (see Abernethy & Kincardine)	90a	Inverness-shire
Kincardine (Ross])	71	Ross & Cromarty
Kincardine O'Neil	209	Aberdeenshire
Kinclaven	365	Perthshire
Kinfauns	366	Perthshire
King Edward	210	Aberdeenshire
Kingarth	555	Buteshire
Kinghorn	439	Fife
Kinglassie	440	Fife
Kingoldrum	295	Angus (Forfarshire)
Kingsbarns	441	Fife
Kingussie & Insh	102	Inverness-shire
Kinloch (see Lethendy)	372	Perthshire
Kinlochspelvie	545	Argyll

Local Authority	Sheriff Court	Commissary Court
Argyll and Bute	Dunoon SC51	Argyll CC2
N. Ayrshire	Rothesay SC8	The Isles CC12
Highland	Inverness SC29	The Isles CC12
Highland	Dingwall SC25	Ross CC19
Argyll & Bute	Dunoon SC51	Argyll CC2
Argyll & Bute	Dunoon SC51	The Isles CC12
Argyll & Bute	Dunoon SC51	Argyll CC2
Fife	Cupar SC20	St Andrews CC20
Perthshire	Perth SC49	St Andrews CC20
N. Lanarkshire	Stirling SC67	Glasgow CC9
Highland	Inverness SC29	Inverness CC11
Highland	Dingwall SC25	Ross CC19
N. Ayrshire	Ayr SC6	Glasgow CC9
Stirling	Perth SC49	Dunblane CC6
Highland	Inverness SC29	Inverness CC11
Highland	Dingwall SC25	Ross CC19
Aberdeenshire	Aberdeen SC1	Aberdeen CC1
Perthshire	Perth SC49	Dunkeld CC7
Perthshire	Perth SC49	St Andrews CC20
Aberdeenshire	Aberdeen SC1	Aberdeen CC1
Argyll & Bute	Rothesay SC8	The Isles CC12
Fife	Cupar SC20	St Andrews CC20
Fife	Cupar SC20	St Andrews CC20
Angus	Forfar SC47	Brechin CC3
Fife	Cupar SC20	St Andrews CC20
Highland	Inverness SC29	Inverness CC11
Perthshire	Perth SC49	Dunkeld CC7
Argyll & Bute	Dunoon SC51	The Isles CC12

Parish	No.	County
Kinloss	138	Morayshire (Elginshire)
Kinnaird	368	Perthshire
Kinneddar (see Drainie)	130	Morayshire (Elginshire)
Kinnell	296	Angus (Forfarshire)
Kinnellar	211	Aberdeenshire
Kinnettles	297	Angus (Forfarshire)
Kinnoir (see Huntly)	202	Aberdeenshire
Kinnoull	369	Perthshire
Kinross	462	Kinross
Kintail	72	Ross & Cromarty
Kintore	213	Aberdeenshire
Kippen	484	Stirlingshire
Kirkbean	870	Kirkcudbrightshire
Kirkcaldy	442	Fife
Kirkcolm	887	Wigtownshire
Kirkconnel	834	Dumfriesshire
Kirkcowan	888	Wigtownshire
Kirkcudbright	871	Kirkcudbrightshire
Kirkden	298	Angus (Forfarshire)
Kirkgunzeon	872	Kirkcudbrightshire
Kirkhill	103	Inverness-shire
Kirkhope	776	Selkirkshire
Kirkinner	889	Wigtownshire
Kirkintilloch	498	Dunbartonshire
Kirkliston	667	W. Lothian (Linlithgowshire)
Kirkmabreck	873	Kirkcudbrightshire
Kirkmahoe	835	Dumfriesshire
Kirkmaiden	890	Wigtownshire
Kirkmichael	370	Perthshire
Kirkmichael (Ayr)	600	Ayrshire

Local Authority	Sheriff Court	Commissary Court
Moray	Elgin SC26	Moray CC16
Perthshire	Perth SC49	St Andrews CC20
Moray	Elgin SC26	Moray CC16
Angus	Forfar SC47	St Andrews CC20
Aberdeenshire	Aberdeen SC1	Aberdeen CC1
Angus	Forfar SC47	St Andrews CC20
Aberdeenshire	Aberdeen SC1	Aberdeen CC1
Perthshire	Perth SC49	St Andrews CC20
Perthshire	Kinross SC22	St Andrews CC20
Highland	Dingwall SC25	Ross CC19
Aberdeenshire	Aberdeen SC1	Aberdeen CC1
Stirling	Stirling SC67	Dunblane CC6
Dumfries & Galloway	Kirkcudbright SC16	Dumfries CC5
Fife	Cupar SC20	St Andrews CC20
Dumfries & Galloway	Wigtown SC19	Wigtown CC22
Dumfries & Galloway	Dumfries SC15	Dumfries CC5
Dumfries & Galloway	Wigtown SC19	Wigtown CC22
Dumfries & Galloway	Kirkcudbright SC16	Kirkcudbright CC13
Angus	Forfar SC47	St Andrews CC20
Dumfries & Galloway	Kirkcudbright SC16	Kirkcudbright CC13
Highland	Inverness SC29	Inverness CC11
The Scottish Borders	Selkirk SC63	Peebles CC18
Dumfries and Galloway	Wigtown SC19	Wigtown CC22
E. Dunbartonshire	Dumbarton SC65	Glasgow CC9
City of Edinburgh	Linlithgow SC41	Edinburgh CC8
Dumfries & Galloway	Kirkcudbright SC16	Kirkcudbright CC13
Dumfries & Galloway	Dumfries SC15	Dumfries CC5
Dumfries & Galloway	Wigtown SC19	Wigtown CC22
Perthshire	Perth SC49	Dunkeld CC7
S. Ayrshire	Ayr SC6	Glasgow CC9

Parish	No.	County
Kirkmichael (Banffshire)	160	Banffshire
Kirkmichael (Dumfries)	836	Dumfriesshire
Kirknewton & East Calder	690	Midlothian (Edinburghshire)
Kirkoswald	601	Ayrshire
Kirkpatrick-Durham	874	Kirkcudbrightshire
Kirkpatrick-Fleming	837	Dumfriesshire
Kirkpatrick-Juxta	838	Dumfriesshire
Kirktown	794	Roxburghshire
Kirkurd	764	Peeblesshire
Kirkwall & St Ola	21	Orkney
Kirriemuir	299	Angus (Forfarshire)
Kishorn (see Applecross)	58	Ross & Cromarty
Knockando	139	Morayshire (Elginshire)
Knockbain (formerly Kilmuir Wester)	73	Ross & Cromarty
Ladykirk	746	Berwickshire
Laggan	104	Inverness-shire
Lairg	53	Sutherland
Lamington & Wandell	659	Lanarkshire
Lanark	648	Lanarkshire
Langholm (Staplegortoun)	839	Dumfriesshire
Langton	747	Berwickshire
Larbert	485	Stirlingshire
Largo	443	Fife
Largs	602	Ayrshire
Lasswade	691	Midlothian (Edinburghshire)
Latheron	38	Caithness
Lauder	748	Berwickshire
Laurencekirk (formerly Conveth)	263	Kincardineshire
Leadhills (see Crawford)	635	Lanarkshire

Local Authority	Sheriff Court	Commissary Court
Moray	Banff SC2	Moray CC16
Dumfries & Galloway	Dumfries SC15	Dumfries CC5
West Lothian	Edinburgh SC70	Edinburgh CC8
South Ayrshire	Ayr SC6	Glasgow CC9
Dumfries & Galloway	Kirkcudbright SC16	Dumfries CC5
Dumfries & Galloway	Dumfries SC15	Dumfries CC5
Dumfries & Galloway	Dumfries SC15	Dumfries CC5
The Scottish Borders	Jedburgh SC62	Peebles CC18
The Scottish Borders	Peebles SC42	Peebles CC18
Orkney	Kirkwall SC11	Orkney & Shetland CC17
Angus	Forfar SC47	St Andrews CC20
Highland	Dingwall SC25	Ross CC19
Moray	Elgin SC26	Moray CC16
Highland	Dingwall SC25	Ross CC19
The Scottish Borders	Duns SC60	Lauder CC15
Highland	Inverness SC29	Inverness CC11
Highland	Dornoch SC9	Caithness CC4
S. Lanarkshire	Lanark SC38	Lanark CC14
S. Lanarkshire	Lanark SC38	Lanark CC14
Dumfries & Galloway	Dumfries SC15	Dumfries CC5
The Scottish Borders	Duns SC60	Lauder CC15
Falkirk	Stirling SC67	Stirling CC21
Fife	Cupar SC20	St Andrews CC20
N. Ayrshire	Ayr SC6	Glasgow CC9
Midlothian	Edinburgh SC70	Edinburgh CC8
Highland	Wick SC14	Caithness CC4
The Scottish Borders	Duns SC60	Lauder CC15
Aberdeenshire	Stonehaven SC5	St Andrews CC20
S. Lanarkshire	Lanark SC38	Lanark CC14

Parish	No.	County
Lecropt	371	Perthshire
Legerwood	749	Berwickshire
Leith – North	692-1	Midlothian (Edinburghshire)
Leith – South	692-2	Midlothian (Edinburghshire)
Leochel – Cushnie	214	Aberdeenshire
Lerwick	5	Zetland
Leslie	215	Aberdeenshire
Leslie	444	Fife
Lesmahagow	649	Lanarkshire
Lessuden (see St Boswells)	804	Roxburghshire
Leswalt	891	Wigtownshire
Lethendy & Kinloch	372	Perthshire
Lethnot & Navar	300	Angus (Forfarshire)
Leuchars	445	Fife
Lhanbryde (see St Andrews)	142	Morayshire (Elginshire)
Libberton	650	Lanarkshire
Liberton	693	Midlothian (Edinburghshire)
Liff, Benvie & Invergowrie	301	Angus (Forfarshire)
Lilliesleaf	795	Roxburghshire
Linlithgow	668	W. Lothian (Linlithgowshire)
Linton	796	Roxburghshire
Lintrathen	302	Angus (Forfarshire)
Lismore & Appin	525	Argyll
Little Dunkeld	373	Perthshire
Livingston	669	W. Lothian (Linlithgowshire)
Lochalsh	74	Ross & Cromarty
Lochbroom	75	Ross & Cromarty
Lochcarron	76	Ross & Cromarty
Lochgoilhead & Kilmorich	527	Argyll

Local Authority	Sheriff Court	Commissary Court
Stirling	Perth SC49	Dunblane CC6
The Scottish Borders	Duns SC60	Lauder CC15
City of Edinburgh	Edinburgh SC70	Edinburgh CC8
City of Edinburgh	Edinburgh SC70	Edinburgh CC8
Aberdeenshire	Aberdeen SC1	Aberdeen CC1
Shetland	Lerwick SC12	Orkney & Shetland CC17
Aberdeenshire	Aberdeen SC1	Aberdeen CC1
Fife	Cupar SC20	Dunkeld CC7
S. Lanarkshire	Lanark SC38	Lanark CC14
The Scottish Borders	Jedburgh SC62	Peebles CC18
Dumfries & Galloway	Wigtown SC19	Wigtown CC22
Perthshire	Perth SC49	Dunkeld CC7
Angus	Forfar SC47	Brechin CC3
Fife	Cupar SC20	St Andrews CC20
Moray	Elgin SC26	Moray CC16
South Lanarkshire	Lanark SC38	Lanark CC14
City of Edinburgh	Edinburgh SC70	Edinburgh CC8
Dundee	Forfar SC47	St Andrews CC20
The Scottish Borders	Jedburgh SC62	Peebles CC18
W. Lothian	Linlithgow SC41	Edinburgh CC8
The Scottish Borders	Jedburgh SC62	Peebles CC18
Angus	Forfar SC47	St Andrews CC20
Argyll & Bute	Dunoon SC51	Argyll CC2
Perthshire	Perth SC49	Dunkeld CC7
W. Lothian	Linlithgow SC41	Edinburgh CC8
Highland	Dingwall SC25	Ross CC19
Highland	Dingwall SC25	Ross CC19
Highland	Dingwall SC25	Ross CC19
Argyll and Bute	Dunoon SC51	Argyll CC2

Parish	No.	County
Lochlee	303	Angus (Forfarshire)
Lochmaben	840	Dumfriesshire
Lochranza (see also Kilmory, 554)	556	Buteshire
Lochrutton	875	Kirkcudbrightshire
Lochs	87	Ross & Cromarty
Lochwinnoch	570	Renfrewshire
Logie	374	Perthshire
Logie (F)	446	Fife
Logie Buchan	216	Aberdeenshire
Logie Coldstone	217	Aberdeenshire
Logie Easter	77	Ross & Cromarty
Logie— Pert	304	Angus (Forfarshire)
Logie Wester (see Urquhart)	84	Ross & Cromarty
Logierait	376	Perthshire
Longforgan	377	Perthshire
Longformacus	750	Berwickshire
Longside	218	Aberdeenshire
Lonmay	219	Aberdeenshire
Loth	54	Sutherland
Loudon	603	Ayrshire
Lumphannan	220	Aberdeenshire
Lunan	305	Angus (Forfarshire)
Lundie & Fowlis	306	Angus (Forfarshire)
Lunnasting (see Nesting)	7	Zetland
Luss	499	Dunbartonshire
Lyne & Megget	765	Peeblesshire
Macduff (see Gamrie)	155a	Banffshire
Madderty	378	Perthshire
Mains & Strathmartine	307	Angus (Forfarshire)
Makerston	797	Roxburghshire

Local Authority	Sheriff Court	Commissary Court
Angus	Forfar SC47	Brechin CC3
Dumfries & Galloway	Dumfries SC15	Dumfries CC5
N. Ayrshire	Rothesay SC8	The Isles CC12
Dumfries & Galloway	Kirkcudbright SC16	Dumfries CC5
Western Isles	Stornoway SC33	The Isles CC12
Renfrewshire	Paisley SC58	Glasgow CC9
Stirling	Perth SC49	Dunblane CC6
Fife	Cupar SC20	St Andrews CC20
Aberdeenshire	Aberdeen SC1	Aberdeen CC1
Aberdeenshire	Aberdeen SC1	Aberdeen CC1
Highland	Dingwall SC25	Ross CC19
Angus	Forfar SC47	St Andrews CC20
Highland	Dingwall SC25	Ross CC19
Perthshire	Perth SC49	Dunkeld CC7
Perthshire	Perth SC49	St Andrews CC20
The Scottish Borders	Duns SC60	Lauder CC15
Aberdeenshire	Aberdeen SC1	Aberdeen CC1
Aberdeenshire	Aberdeen SC1	Aberdeen CC1
Highland	Dornoch SC9	Caithness CC4
E. Ayrshire	Ayr SC6	Glasgow CC9
Aberdeenshire	Aberdeen SC1	Aberdeen CC1
Angus	Forfar SC47	St Andrews CC20
Angus	Forfar SC47	St Andrews CC20
Shetland	Lerwick SC12	Orkney & Shetland CC17
Argyll & Bute	Dumbarton SC65	Glasgow CC9
The Scottish Borders	Peebles SC42	Peebles CC18
Aberdeenshire	Banff SC2	Aberdeen CC1
Perthshire	Perth SC49	Dunkeld CC7
Dundee	Forfar SC47	St Andrews CC20
The Scottish Borders	Jedburgh SC62	Peebles CC18

Parish	No.	County
Manor	766	Peeblesshire
Markinch	447	Fife
Marnoch	161	Banffshire
Maryculter	264	Kincardineshire
Marykirk (formerly Aberluthnot)	265	Kincardineshire
Maryton	308	Angus (Forfarshire)
Mauchline	604	Ayrshire
Maxton	798	Roxburghshire
Maxwelltown (see Troqueer)	882	Kirkcudbrightshire
Maybole	605	Ayrshire
Mearns	571	Renfrewshire
Megget (see Lyne)	765	Peeblesshire
Meigle	379	Perthshire
Meldrum (see Oldmeldrum)	229	Aberdeenshire
Melrose	799	Roxburghshire
Menmuir	309	Angus (Forfarshire)
Mertoun	751	Berwickshire
Methlick	221	Aberdeenshire
Methven	380	Perthshire
Mid & South Yell	6	Zetland
Mid-Calder	694	Midlothian (Edinburghshire)
Middlebie	841	Dumfriesshire
Midmar	222	Aberdeenshire
Minnigaff	876	Kirkcudbrightshire
Minto	800	Roxburghshire
Mochrum	892	Wigtownshire
Moffat	842	Dumfriesshire
Moneydie	381	Perthshire
Monifieth	310	Angus (Forfarshire)
Monikie	311	Angus (Forfarshire)

Local Authority	Sheriff Court	Commissary Court
The Scottish Borders	Peebles SC42	Peebles CC18
Fife	Cupar SC20	St Andrews CC20
Aberdeenshire	Banff SC2	Moray CC16
Aberdeenshire	Stonehaven SC5	Aberdeen CC1
Aberdeenshire	Stonehaven SC5	St Andrews CC20
Angus	Forfar SC47	Brechin CC3
E. Ayrshire	Ayr SC6	Glasgow CC9
The Scottish Borders	Jedburgh SC62	Peebles CC18
Dumfries & Galloway	Kirkcudbright SC16	Kirkcudbright CC13
S. Ayrshire	Ayr SC6	Glasgow CC9
E. Renfrewshire	Paisley SC58	Glasgow CC9
The Scottish Borders	Peebles SC42	Peebles CC18
Perthshire	Perth SC49	Dunkeld CC7
Aberdeenshire	Aberdeen SC1	Aberdeen CC1
The Scottish Borders	Jedburgh SC62	Peebles CC18
Angus	Forfar SC47	Brechin CC3
The Scottish Borders	Duns SC60	Lauder CC15
Aberdeenshire	Aberdeen SC1	Aberdeen CC1
Perthshire	Perth SC49	St Andrews CC20
Shetland	Lerwick SC12	Orkney & Shetland CC17
W. Lothian	Edinburgh SC70	Edinburgh CC8
Dumfries & Galloway	Dumfries SC15	Dumfries CC5
Aberdeenshire	Aberdeen SC1	Aberdeen CC1
Dumfries & Galloway	Kirkcudbright SC16	Wigtown CC22
The Scottish Borders	Jedburgh SC62	Peebles CC18
Dumfries & Galloway	Wigtown SC19	Wigtown CC22
Dumfries & Galloway	Dumfries SC15	Dumfries CC5
Perthshire	Perth SC49	Dunkeld CC7
Angus/Dundee	Forfar SC47	St Andrews CC20
Angus	Forfar SC47	Brechin CC3

Parish	No.	County
Monimail	448	Fife
Monkton & Prestwick	606	Ayrshire
Monquhitter	223	Aberdeenshire
Montrose	312	Angus (Forfarshire)
Monyabroch (see Kilsyth)	483	Stirlingshire
Monymusk	224	Aberdeenshire
Monzie	382	Perthshire
Monzievaird & Strowan	383	Perthshire
Moonzie	449	Fife
Mordington	752	Berwickshire
Morebattle	801	Roxburghshire
Morham	712	E. Lothian (Haddingtonshire)
Mortlach	162	Banffshire
Morton	843	Dumfriesshire
Morvern	528	Argyll
Moulin	384	Perthshire
Mouswald	844	Dumfriesshire
Moy & Dalarossie	105	Invernessshire
Muckairn	529	Argyll
Muckhart	385	Perthshire
Muiravonside	486	Stirlingshire
Muirkirk	607	Ayrshire
Murroes	313	Angus (Forfarshire)
Muthill	386a	Perthshire
Nairn	123	Nairnshire
Neilston	572	Renfrewshire
Nenthorn	753	Berwickshire
Nesting	7	Zetland
New Abbey	877	Kirkcudbrightshire
New Cumnock	608	Ayrshire

Local Authority	Sheriff Court	Commissary Court
Fife	Cupar SC20	St Andrews CC20
South Ayrshire	Ayr SC6	Glasgow CC9
Aberdeenshire	Aberdeen SC1	Aberdeen CC1
Angus	Forfar SC47	Brechin CC3
Aberdeenshire	Aberdeen SC1	Aberdeen CC1
Perthshire	Perth SC49	Dunblane CC6
Perthshire	Perth SC49	Dunblane CC6
Fife	Cupar SC20	St Andrews CC20
The Scottish Borders	Duns SC60	Lauder CC15
The Scottish Borders	Jedburgh SC62	Peebles CC18
E. Lothian	Haddington SC40	Edinburgh CC8
Moray	Banff SC2	Aberdeen CC1
Dumfries & Galloway	Dumfries SC15	Dumfries CC5
Highland	Dunoon SC51	Argyll CC2
Perthshire	Perth SC49	Dunkeld CC7
Dumfries & Galloway	Dumfries SC15	Dumfries CC5
Highland	Inverness SC29	Inverness CC11
Argyll & Bute	Dunoon SC51	Argyll CC2
Clackmannan	Perth SC49	St Andrews CC20
Falkirk	Stirling SC67	Stirling CC21
E. Ayrshire	Ayr SC6	Glasgow CC9
Dundee	Forfar SC47	St Andrews CC20
Perthshire	Perth SC49	Dunblane CC6
Highland	Nairn SC31	Moray CC16
E. Renfrewshire	Paisley SC58	Glasgow CC9
The Scottish Borders	Duns SC60	Lauder CC15
Shetland	Lerwick SC12	Orkney & Shetland CC17
Dumfries & Galloway	Kirkcudbright SC16	Dumfries CC5
E. Ayrshire	Ayr SC6	Glasgow CC9

Parish	No.	County
New Deer	225	Aberdeenshire
New Kilpatrick	500	Dunbartonshire
New Luce	893	Wigtownshire
New Machar	227	Aberdeenshire
New Monkland	651	Lanarkshire
New Spynie	136	Morayshire (Elginshire)
Newbattle	695	Midlothian (Edinburghshire)
Newburgh	450	Fife
Newburn	451	Fife
Newhills	226	Aberdeenshire
Newlands	767	Peeblesshire
Newton	696	Midlothian (Edinburghshire)
Newton upon Ayr (see St Quivox)	612	Ayrshire
Newtyle	314	Angus (Forfarshire)
Nigg	78	Ross & Cromarty
Nigg	266	Kincardineshire
North Berwick	713	E. Lothian (Haddingtonshire)
North Bute	557	Buteshire
North Knapdale	530	Argyll
North Ronaldsay	22	Orkney
North Uist	113	Invernessshire
Northmavine	8	Zetland
Oa	546	Argyll
Oathlaw	315	Angus (Forfarshire)
Ochiltree	609	Ayrshire
Old Cumnock	610	Ayrshire
Old Deer	228	Aberdeenshire
Old Kilpatrick	501	Dunbartonshire
Old Luce (Glenluce)	894	Wigtownshire
Old Machar	168b	Aberdeenshire

Local Authority	Sheriff Court	Commissary Court
Aberdeenshire	Aberdeen SC1	Aberdeen CC1
E. Dunbartonshire	Dumbarton SC65	Glasgow CC9
Dumfries & Galloway	Wigtown SC19	Wigtown CC22
Aberdeenshire	Aberdeen SC1	Aberdeen CC1
N. Lanarkshire	Hamilton SC37	Hamilton & Campsie CC10
Moray	Elgin SC26	Moray CC16
Midlothian	Edinburgh SC70	Edinburgh CC8
Fife	Cupar SC20	St Andrews CC20
Fife	Cupar SC20	St Andrews CC20
Aberdeenshire	Aberdeen SC1	Aberdeen CC1
The Scottish Borders	Peebles SC42	Peebles CC18
Midlothian	Edinburgh SC70	Edinburgh CC8
S. Ayrshire	Ayr SC6	Glasgow CC9
Angus	Forfar SC47	St Andrews CC20
Highland	Dingwall SC25	Ross CC19
Aberdeen City	Stonehaven SC5	St Andrews CC20
E. Lothian	Haddington SC40	Edinburgh CC8
Argyll & Bute	Rothesay SC8	The Isles CC12
Argyll & Bute	Dunoon SC51	Argyll CC2
Orkney	Kirkwall SC11	Orkney & Shetland CC17
Western Isles	Inverness SC29	The Isles CC12
Shetland	Lerwick SC12	Orkney & Shetland CC17
Argyll & Bute	Dunoon SC51	The Isles CC12
Angus	Forfar SC47	Brechin CC3
E. Ayrshire	Ayr SC6	Glasgow CC9
E. Ayrshire	Ayr SC6	Glasgow CC9
Aberdeenshire	Aberdeen SC1	Aberdeen CC1
W. Dunbartonshire	Dumbarton SC65	Glasgow CC9
Dumfries & Galloway	Wigtown SC19	Wigtown CC22
Aberdeen City	Aberdeen SC1	Aberdeen CC1

APPENDICES

Parish	No.	County
Old Monkland	652	Lanarkshire
Oldhamstocks	714	E. Lothian (Haddingtonshire)
Oldmeldrum (Meldrum)	229	Aberdeenshire
Olrig	39	Caithness
Ordiquhill	163	Banffshire
Ormiston	715	E. Lothian (Haddingtonshire)
Orphir	23	Orkney
Orwell	463	Kinross
Oxnam	802	Roxburghshire
Oyne	230	Aberdeenshire
Paisley (High, Middle & Low)	573	Renfrewshire
Panbride	316	Angus (Forfarshire)
Papa Westray	33	Orkney
Parton	878	Kirkcudbrightshire
Peebles	768	Peeblesshire
Pencaitland	716	E. Lothian (Haddingtonshire)
Penicuik	697	Midlothian (Edinburghshire)
Penninghame	895	Wigtownshire
Penpont	845	Dumfriesshire
Perth	387	Perthshire
Peterculter	231	Aberdeenshire
Peterhead	232	Aberdeenshire
Pettinain	653	Lanarkshire
Petty	106	Invernessshire
Pitsligo	233	Aberdeenshire
Pittenweem	452	Fife
Polmont	487	Stirlingshire
Polwarth	754	Berwickshire
Poolewe (see Gairloch)	66	Ross & Cromarty
Port Glasgow	574	Renfrewshire

Local Authority	Sheriff Court	Commissary Court
N. Lanarkshire	Hamilton SC37	Hamilton & Campsie CC10
E. Lothian	Haddington SC40	Edinburgh CC8
Aberdeenshire	Aberdeen SC1	Aberdeen CC1
Highland	Wick SC14	Caithness CC4
Aberdeenshire	Banff SC2	Aberdeen CC1
E. Lothian	Haddington SC40	Edinburgh CC8
Orkney	Kirkwall SC11	Orkney & Shetland CC17
Perthshire	Kinross SC22	St Andrews CC20
The Scottish Borders	Jedburgh SC62	Peebles CC18
Aberdeenshire	Aberdeen SC1	Aberdeen CC1
Renfrewshire	Paisley SC58	Glasgow CC9
Angus	Forfar SC47	Brechin CC3
Orkney	Kirkwall .SC11	Orkney & Shetland CC17
Dumfries & Galloway	Kirkcudbright SC16	Kirkcudbright CC13
The Scottish Borders	Peebles SC42	Peebles CC18
E. Lothian	Haddington SC40	Edinburgh CC8
Midlothian	Edinburgh SC70	Edinburgh CC8
Dumfries & Galloway	Wigtown SC19	Wigtown CC22
Dumfries & Galloway	Dumfries SC15	Dumfries CC5
Perthshire	Perth SC49	St Andrews CC20
Aberdeen City	Aberdeen SC1	Aberdeen CC1
Aberdeenshire	Aberdeen SC1	Aberdeen CC1
S. Lanarkshire	Lanark SC38	Lanark CC14
Highland	Inverness SC29	Moray CC16
Aberdeenshire	Aberdeen SC1	Aberdeen CC1
Fife	Cupar SC20	St Andrews CC20
Falkirk	Stirling SC67	Stirling CC21
The Scottish Borders	Duns SC60	Lauder CC15
Highland	Dingwall SC25	Ross CC19
Inverclyde	Paisley SC58	Glasgow CC9

Parish	No.	County
Port of Menteith	388	Perthshire
Portmoak	464	Kinross
Portnahaven	547	Argyll
Portpatrick	896	Wigtownshire
Portree	114	Invernessshire
Premnay	234	Aberdeenshire
Prestonhaugh	717	E. Lothian (Haddingtonshire)
Prestonkirk	717	E. Lothian (Haddingtonshire)
Prestonpans	718	E. Lothian (Haddingtonshire)
Prestwick (see Monkton)	606	Ayrshire
Queensferry	670	W. Lothian (Linlithgowshire)
Rafford	140	Morayshire (Elginshire)
Rathen	235	Aberdeenshire
Ratho	698a	Midlothian (Edinburghshire)
Rathven	164	Banffshire
Rattray	389	Perthshire
Rayne	236	Aberdeenshire
Reay	40	Caithness
Redgorton	390	Perthshire
Renfrew	575	Renfrewshire
Rerrick	879	Kirkcudbrightshire
Rescobie	317	Angus (Forfarshire)
Resolis	79	Ross & Cromarty
(formerly Kirkmichael & Cullicudden)		
Rhynd	391	Perthshire
Rhynie (includes Essie)	237A	Aberdeenshire
Riccarton	611	Ayrshire
Roberton	777	Selkirkshire
Roberton (Lanarks.)(see Wiston)	660	Lanarkshire

Local Authority	Sheriff Court	Commissary Court
Stirling	Perth SC49	Dunblane CC6
Perthshire	Kinross SC22	St Andrews CC20
Argyll and Bute	Dunoon SC51	The Isles CC12
Dumfries & Galloway	Wigtown SC19	Wigtown CC22
Highland	Inverness SC29	The Isles CC12
Aberdeenshire	Aberdeen SC1	Aberdeen CC1
E. Lothian	Haddington SC40	Edinburgh CC8
E. Lothian	Haddington SC40	Edinburgh CC8
E. Lothian	Haddington SC40	Edinburgh CC8
S. Ayrshire	Ayr SC6	Glasgow CC9
City of Edinburgh	Linlithgow SC41	Edinburgh CC8
Moray	Elgin SC26	Moray CC16
Aberdeenshire	Aberdeen SC1	Aberdeen CC1
City of Edinburgh	Edinburgh SC70	Edinburgh CC8
Moray	Banff SC2	Aberdeen CC1
Perthshire	Perth SC49	Dunkeld CC7
Aberdeenshire	Aberdeen SC1	Aberdeen CC1
Highland	Wick SC14	Caithness CC4
Perthshire	Perth SC49	Dunkeld CC7
Renfrewshire	Paisley SC58	Hamilton & Campsie CC10
Dumfries & Galloway	Kirkcudbright SC16	Kirkcudbright CC13
Angus	Forfar SC47	St Andrews CC20
Highland	Dingwall SC25	Ross CC19
Perthshire	Perth SC49	St Andrews CC20
Aberdeenshire	Aberdeen SC1	Moray CC16
E.Ayrshire	Ayr SC6	Glasgow CC9
The Scottish Borders	Selkirk SC63	Peebles CC18
S. Lanarkshire	Lanark SC38	Lanark CC14

Parish	No.	County
Rogart	55	Sutherland
Rosemarkie	80	Ross & Cromarty
Roseneath	502	Dunbartonshire
Rosskeen	81	Ross & Cromarty
Rothes (incl Dundurcas)	141	Morayshire (Elginshire)
Rothesay	558	Buteshire
Rothiemay	165	Banffshire
Rothiemurcus (see Duthil)	96b	Invernessshire
Rousay & Egilsay	24	Orkney
Row (Rhu)	503	Dunbartonshire
Roxburgh	803	Roxburghshire
Rutherglen	654	Lanarkshire
Ruthven	318	Angus (Forfarshire)
Ruthwell	846	Dumfriesshire
Saddell & Skipness	531	Argyll
Saline	455	Fife
Saltoun	719	E. Lothian (Haddingtonshire)
Saltpreston (see Prestonpans)	718	E. Lothian (Haddingtonshire
Sanday	26	Orkney
Sandsting & Aithsting	9	Zetland
Sandwick	27	Orkney
Sandwick (see Dunrossness)	3	Zetland
Sanquhar	848	Dumfriesshire
Savoch	237B	Aberdeenshire
Scone	394a	Perthshire
Scoonie	456	Fife
Selkirk	778	Selkirkshire
Shapinsay	28	Orkney
Shieldaig (see Applecross)	58	Ross & Cromarty
Shisken (see Kilmory)	554	Buteshire

Local Authority	Sheriff Court	Commissary Court
Highland	Dornoch SC9	Caithness CC4
Highland	Dingwall SC25	Ross CC19
Argyll & Bute	Dumbarton SC65	Glasgow CC9
Highland	Dingwall SC25	Ross CC19
Moray	Elgin SC26	Moray CC16
Argyll & Bute	Rothesay SC8	The Isles CC12
Moray	Banff SC2	Moray CC16
Highland	Inverness SC29	Inverness CC11
Orkney	Kirkwall SC11	Orkney & Shetland CC17
Argyll & Bute	Dumbarton SC65	Glasgow CC9
The Scottish Borders	Jedburgh SC62	Peebles CC18
S. Lanarkshire	Glasgow SC36	Glasgow CC9
Angus	Forfar SC47	Dunkeld CC7
Dumfries & Galloway	Dumfries SC15	Dumfries CC5
Argyll & Bute	Dunoon SC51	Argyll CC2
Fife	Cupar SC20	Stirling CC21
E. Lothian	Haddington SC40	Edinburgh CC8
E. Lothian	Haddington SC40	Edinburgh CC8
Orkney	Kirkwall SC11	Orkney & Shetland CC17
Shetland	Lerwick SC12	Orkney & Shetland CC17
Orkney	Kirkwall SC11	Orkney & Shetland CC17
Shetland	Lerwick SC12	Orkney & Shetland CC17
Dumfries & Galloway	Dumfries SC15	Dumfries CC5
Aberdeenshire	Aberdeen SC1	Aberdeen CC1
Perthshire	Perth SC49	St Andrews CC20
Fife	Cupar SC20	St Andrews CC20
The Scottish Borders	Selkirk SC63	Peebles CC18
Orkney	Kirkwall SC11	Orkney & Shetland CC17
Highland	Dingwall SC25	Ross CC19
N. Ayrshire	Rothesay SC8	The Isles CC12

Parish	No.	County
Shotts	655	Lanarkshire
Skene	238	Aberdeenshire
Skerries (see Nesting)	7	Zetland
Skipness (see Saddell & Skipness)	531	Argyll
Skirling	769	Peeblesshire
Slains	239	Aberdeenshire
Slamannan	489	Stirlingshire
Sleat	115	Inverness-shire
Smailholm	805	Roxburghshire
Small Isles	116	Inverness-sshire (Argyll)
Snizort	117	Inverness-shire
Sorbie	897	Wigtownshire
Sorn (formerly Dalgain)	613	Ayrshire
South Knapdale	533	Argyll
South Ronaldsay & Burray	29	Orkney
South Uist	118	Inverness-shire
Southdean & Abbotrule	806	
Southend	532	Argyll
Speymouth (formerly Essil & Dipple)	143	Morayshire (Elginshire)
Spott	720	E. Lothian (Haddingtonshire)
Sprouston	807	Roxburghshire
St Andrews & St Leonards	453	Fife
St Andrews (incl Lhanbryde)	142	Morayshire (Elginshire)
St Andrews (Orkney)	25	Orkney
St Boswells	804	Roxburghshire
St Cyrus (formerly Ecclesgreig)	267	Kincardineshire
St Fergus	166	Aberdeenshire (orig. Banffshire)
St Kilda (see Harris)	111	Invernessshire
St Madoes	392	Perthshire

Local Authority	Sheriff Court	Commissary Court
N. Lanarkshire	Hamilton SC37	Hamilton & Campsie CC10
Aberdeenshire	Aberdeen SC1	Aberdeen CC1
Shetland	Lerwick SC12	Orkney & Shetland CC17
Argyll & Bute	Dunoon SC51	Argyll CC2
The Scottish Borders	Peebles SC42	Peebles CC18
Aberdeenshire	Aberdeen SC1	Aberdeen CC1
Falkirk	Stirling SC67	Stirling CC21
Highland	Inverness SC29	The Isles CC12
The Scottish Borders	Jedburgh SC62	Peebles CC18
Highland	Inverness SC29	The Isles CC12
Highland	Inverness SC29	The Isles CC12
Dumfries & Galloway	Wigtown SC19	Wigtown CC22
E. Ayrshire	Ayr SC6	Glasgow CC9
Argyll & Bute	Dunoon SC51	Argyll CC2
Orkney	Kirkwall SC11	Orkney & Shetland CC17
Western Isles	Inverness SC29	The Isles CC12
The Scottish Borders	Jedburgh SC62	Peebles CC18
Argyll & Bute	Dunoon SC51	Argyll CC2
Moray	Elgin SC26	Moray CC16
E. Lothian	Haddington SC40	Edinburgh CC8
The Scottish Borders	Jedburgh SC62	Peebles CC18
Fife	Cupar SC20	St Andrews CC20
Moray	Elgin SC26	Moray CC16
Orkney	Kirkwall SC11	Orkney & Shetland CC17
The Scottish Borders	Jedburgh SC62	Peebles CC18
Aberdeenshire	Stonehaven SC5	St Andrews CC20
Aberdeenshire	Aberdeen SC1	Aberdeen CC1
Western Isles	Inverness SC29	The Isles CC12
Perthshire	Perth SC49	Dunblane CC6

Parish	No.	County
St Martins	393	Perthshire
St Monance (or Abercrombie)	454	Fife
St Mungo	847	Dumfriesshire
St Ninians	488	Stirlingshire
St Quivox & Newton upon Ayr	612	Ayrshire
St Vigeans	319	Angus (Forfarshire)
Stair	614	Ayrshire
Staplegordon (see Langholm)	839	Dumfriesshire
Stenness (see Firth)	17	Orkney
Stenton	721	E. Lothian (Haddingtonshire)
Stevenston	615	Ayrshire
Stewarton	616	Ayrshire
Stirling	490	Stirlingshire
Stitchel & Hume	808	Roxburghshire
Stobo	770	Peeblesshire
Stonehouse	656	Lanarkshire
Stoneykirk	898	Wigtownshire
Stornoway	88	Ross & Cromarty
Stow	699	Midlothian (Edinburghshire)
Stracathro	320	Angus (Forfarshire)
Strachan	268	Kincardineshire
Strachur & Stralachlan	534	Argyll
Straiton	617	Ayrshire
Stralachlan	534	Argyll
(see Strachur & Stralachlan)		
Stranraer	899	Wigtownshire
Strath	119	Invernessshire
Strathblane	491	Stirlingshire
Strathdon (includes Corgarff)	240	Aberdeenshire

Local Authority	Sheriff Court	Commissary Court
Perthshire	Perth SC49	Dunkeld CC7
Fife	Cupar SC20	St Andrews CC20
Dumfries & Galloway	Dumfries SC15	Dumfries CC5
Stirling	Stirling SC67	Stirling CC21
S. Ayrshire	Ayr SC6	Glasgow CC9
Angus	Forfar SC47	St Andrews CC20
E. Ayrshire	Ayr SC6	Glasgow CC9
Dumfries & Galloway	Dumfries SC15	Dumfries CC5
Orkney	Kirkwall SC11	Orkney & Shetland CC17
E. Lothian	Haddington SC40	Edinburgh CC8
N. Ayrshire	Ayr SC6	Glasgow CC9
E. Ayrshire	Ayr SC6	Glasgow CC9
Stirling	Stirling SC67	Stirling CC21
The Scottish Borders	Jedburgh SC62	Peebles CC18
The Scottish Borders	Peebles SC42	Peebles CC18
S. Lanarkshire	Hamilton SC37	Glasgow CC9
Dumfries & Galloway	Wigtown SC19	Wigtown CC22
Western Isles	Stornoway SC33	The Isles CC12
The Scottish Borders	Edinburgh SC70	Edinburgh CC8
Angus	Forfar SC47	Brechin CC3
Aberdeenshire	Stonehaven SC5	Brechin CC3
Argyll & Bute	Dunoon SC51	Argyll CC2
South Ayrshire	Ayr SC6	Glasgow CC9
Argyll & Bute	Dunoon SC51	Argyll CC2
Dumfries & Galloway	Wigtown SC19	Wigtown CC22
Highland	Inverness SC29	The Isles CC12
Stirlingshire	Stirling SC67	Glasgow CC9
Aberdeenshire	Aberdeen SC1	Aberdeen CC1

Parish	No.	County
Strathmiglo	457	Fife
Strichen	241	Aberdeenshire
Stromness	30	Orkney
Stronsay	31	Orkney
Strontian (Islandfinnan) (see Ardnamurchan)	505	Argyll
Swinton (incl Simprim)	755	Berwickshire
Symington	618	Ayrshire
Symington (Lanarks.)	657	Lanarkshire
Tain	82	Ross & Cromarty
Tannadice	321	Angus (Forfarshire)
Tarbat	83	Ross & Cromarty
Tarbolton	619	Ayrshire
Tarland & Migvie	242	Aberdeenshire
Tarves	243	Aberdeenshire
Tealing	322	Angus (Forfarshire)
Temple	700	Midlothian (Edinburghshire)
Terregles	880	Kirkcudbrightshire
Teviothead	809	Roxburghshire
Thankerton (see Covington & Thankerton)	634	Lanarkshire
Thurso	41	Caithness
Tibbermore	395	Perthshire
Tillicoultry	468	Clackmannanshire
Tingwall	10	Zetland
Tinwald	849	Dumfriesshire
Tiree (incl Coll)	551	Argyll
Tongland	881	Kirkcudbrightshire
Tongue	56	Sutherland
Torosay	550	Argyll

Local Authority	Sheriff Court	Commissary Court
Fife	Cupar SC20	Dunkeld CC7
Aberdeenshire	Aberdeen SC1	Aberdeen CC1
Orkney	Kirkwall SC11	Orkney & Shetland CC17
Orkney	Kirkwall SC11	Orkney & Shetland CC17
Highland	Dunoon SC51	Argyll CC2
The Scottish Borders	Duns SC60	Lauder CC15
South Ayrshire	Ayr SC6	Glasgow CC9
S. Lanarkshire	Lanark SC38	Lanark CC14
Highland	Dingwall SC25	Ross CC19
Angus	Forfar SC47	St Andrews CC20
Highland	Dingwall SC25	Ross CC19
South Ayrshire	Ayr SC6	Glasgow CC9
Aberdeenshire	Aberdeen SC1	Aberdeen CC1
Aberdeenshire	Aberdeen SC1	Aberdeen CC1
Angus	Forfar SC47	Dunkeld CC7
Midlothian	Edinburgh SC70	Edinburgh CC8
Dumfries & Galloway	Kirkcudbright SC16	Dumfries CC5
The Scottish Borders	Jedburgh SC62	Peebles CC18
S. Lanarkshire	Lanark SC38	Lanark CC14
Highland	Wick SC14	Caithness CC4
Perthshire	Perth SC49	Dunkeld CC7
Clackmannan	Alloa SC64	Dunblane CC6
Shetland	Lerwick SC12	Orkney & Shetland CC17
Dumfries & Galloway	Dumfries SC15	Dumfries CC5
Argyll & Bute	Dunoon SC51	The Isles CC12
Dumfries & Galloway	Kirkcudbright SC16	Kirkcudbright CC13
Highland	Dornoch SC9	Caithness CC4
Argyll & Bute	Dunoon SC51	The Isles CC12

Parish	No.	County
Torphichen	671	West Lothian (Linlithgowshire)
Torryburn	458	Fife
Torthorwald	850	Dumfriesshire
Tough	244	Aberdeenshire
Towie	245	Aberdeenshire
Tranent	722	E. Lothian (Haddingtonshire)
Traquair	771	Peeblesshire
Trinity Gask	396	Perthshire
Troqueer	882	Kirkcudbrightshire
Tulliallan	397	Perthshire (later Fife)
Tullynessle & Forbes	246	Aberdeenshire
Tundergarth	851	Dumfriesshire
Turriff	247	Aberdeenshire
Tweedsmuir	772	Peeblesshire
Twynholm	883	Kirkcudbrightshire
Tyninghame (see Whitekirk)	723	East Lothian (Haddingtonshire)
Tynron	852	Dumfriesshire
Tyrie	248	Aberdeenshire
Udny	249	Aberdeenshire
Uig	89	Ross & Cromarty
Unst	11	Zetland
Uphall	672	W. Lothian (Linlithgowshire)
Urquhart	144	Morayshire (Elginshire)
Urquhart & Glenmoriston	107	Invernessshire
Urquhart & Logie Wester	84	Ross & Cromarty
Urr	884	Kirkcudbrightshire
Urray	85	Ross & Cromarty
Walls	12	Zetland
Walls (incl. Flotta)	32	Orkney
Walston	658	Lanarkshire

Local Authority	Sheriff Court	Commissary Court
West Lothian	Linlithgow SC41	Edinburgh CC8
Fife	Cupar SC20	Stirling CC21
Dumfries & Galloway	Dumfries SC15	Dumfries CC5
Aberdeenshire	Aberdeen SC1	Aberdeen CC1
Aberdeenshire	Aberdeen SC1	Aberdeen CC1
E. Lothian	Haddington SC40	Edinburgh CC8
The Scottish Borders	Peebles SC42	Peebles CC18
Perthshire	Perth SC49	Dunblane CC6
Dumfries & Galloway	Kirkcudbright SC16	Dumfries CC5
Fife	Perth SC49	Dunblane CC6
Aberdeenshire	Aberdeen SC1	Aberdeen CC1
Dumfries & Galloway	Dumfries SC15	Dumfries CC5
Aberdeenshire	Aberdeen SC1	Aberdeen CC1
The Scottish Borders	Peebles SC42	Peebles CC18
Dumfries & Galloway	Kirkcudbright SC16	Kirkcudbright CC13
East Lothian	Haddington SC40	Edinburgh CC8
Dumfries & Galloway	Dumfries SC15	Dumfries CC5
Aberdeenshire	Aberdeen SC1	Aberdeen CC1
Aberdeenshire	Aberdeen SC1	Aberdeen CC1
Western Isles	Stornoway SC33	The Isles CC12
Shetland	Lerwick SC12	Orkney & Shetland CC17
W. Lothian	Linlithgow SC41	Edinburgh CC8
Moray	Elgin SC26	Moray CC16
Highland	Inverness SC29	Inverness CC11
Highland	Dingwall SC25	Ross CC19
Dumfries & Galloway	Kirkcudbright SC16	Kirkcudbright CC13
Highland	Dingwall SC25	Ross CC19
Shetland	Lerwick SC12	Orkney & Shetland CC17
Orkney	Kirkwall SC11	Orkney & Shetland CC17
S. Lanarkshire	Lanark SC38	Lanark CC14

Parish	No.	County
Wamphray	853a	Dumfriesshire
Wandell & Lamington	659	Lanarkshire
Watten	42	Caithness
Weem	398	Perthshire
Weisdale (see Tingwall)	10	Zetland
Wemyss	459	Fife
West Calder	701	Midlothian (Edinburghshire)
West Kilbride	620	Ayrshire
West Linton	773	Peeblesshire
Westerkirk	854	Dumfriesshire
Westray (incl. Papa Westray)	33	Orkney
Westruther	756	Berwickshire
Whalsay (see Nesting)	7	Zetland
Whitburn	673	W. Lothian (Linlithgowshire)
Whitekirk & Tyninghame	723	E. Lothian (Haddingtonshire)
Whiteness (see Tingwall)	10	Zetland
Whithorn	900	Wigtownshire
Whitsome & Hilton	757	Berwickshire
Whittinghame	724	East Lothian (Haddingtonshire)
Wick	43	Caithness
Wigtown	901	Wigtownshire
Wilton	810	Roxburghshire
Wiston & Roberton	660	Lanarkshire
Yarrow	779	Selkirkshire
Yester	725	East Lothian (Haddingtonshire)
Yetholm	811	Roxburghshire

Local Authority	Sheriff Court	Commissary Court
Dumfries & Galloway	Dumfries SC15	Dumfries CC5
S. Lanarkshire	Lanark SC38	Lanark CC14
Highland	Wick SC14	Caithness CC4
Perthshire	Perth SC49	Dunkeld CC7
Shetland	Lerwick SC12	Orkney & Shetland CC17
Fife	Cupar SC20	St Andrews CC20
W. Lothian	Edinburgh SC70	Edinburgh CC8
N. Ayrshire	Ayr SC6	Glasgow CC9
The Scottish Borders	Peebles SC42	Peebles CC18
Dumfries & Galloway	Dumfries SC15	Dumfries CC5
Orkney	Kirkwall SC11	Orkney & Shetland CC17
The Scottish Borders	Duns SC60	Lauder CC15
Shetland	Lerwick SC12	Orkney & Shetland CC17
W. Lothian	Linlithgow SC41	Edinburgh CC8
E. Lothian	Haddington SC40	Edinburgh CC8
Shetland	Lerwick SC12	Orkney & Shetland CC17
Dumfries & Galloway	Wigtown SC19	Wigtown CC22
The Scottish Borders	Duns SC60	Lauder CC15
East Lothian	Haddington SC40	Edinburgh CC8
Highland	Wick SC14	Caithness CC4
Dumfries & Galloway	Wigtown SC19	Wigtown CC22
The Scottish Borders	Jedburgh SC62	Peebles CC18
South Lanarkshire	Lanark SC38	Lanark CC14
The Scottish Borders	Selkirk SC63	Peebles CC18
East Lothian	Haddington SC40	Edinburgh CC8
The Scottish Borders	Jedburgh SC62	Peebles CC18

Forfeited estate papers

Franchise Court

Protocol books

General Register of Sasines

Burgh

LAND RECORDS, RENTALS & SASINES

Barony

Particular Register of Sasines

Treasury

Family papers

Chancery (Retours)

Register of the Great Seal

Sources for Land Ownership and Land Occupation

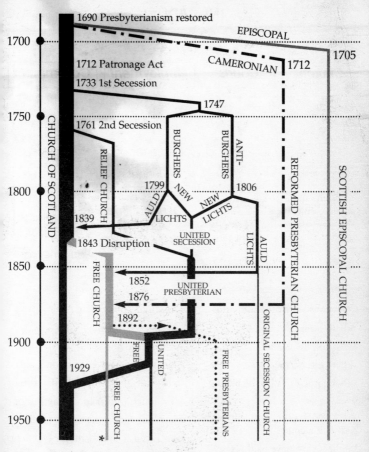

1690 Presbyterianism restored

EPISCOPAL

1700

1705

1712 Patronage Act

CAMERONIAN 1712

1733 1st Secession

1747

1750

1761 2nd Secession

CHURCH OF SCOTLAND

BURGHERS

ANTI-BURGHERS

RELIEF CHURCH

REFORMED PRESBYTERIAN CHURCH

SCOTTISH EPISCOPAL CHURCH

1799 NEW

1806

1800

AULD NEW LICHTS

LICHTS

1839

UNITED SECESSION

AULD LICHTS

1843 Disruption

FREE CHURCH

1850

1852

1876

UNITED PRESBYTERIAN

ORIGINAL SECESSION CHURCH

1892

FREE PRESBYTERIANS

1900

FREE

UNITED

1929

FREE CHURCH

1950

*

* In 2000, the Free Church was split once again following the
breakaway of the Free Church (Continuing) congregations

Secessions from and Disruption of the Church of Scotland

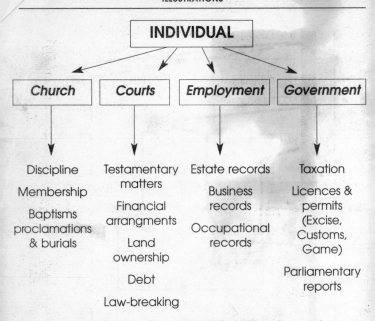

INDIVIDUAL

Church | **Courts** | **Employment** | **Government**

Discipline

Membership

Baptisms proclamations & burials

Testamentary matters

Financial arrangments

Land ownership

Debt

Law-breaking

Estate records

Business records

Occupational records

Taxation

Licences & permits (Excise, Customs, Game)

Parliamentary reports

Questions about the individual:

When did he/she live?

What did he/she do?

Where did he/she live?

What church did he/she belong to?

What contact might he/she have had with a court?

Might he/she have paid taxes?

Questions about the records:

Where do I find the record?

Is the record accessible?

Does it have indexes or finding aids?

What sort of information may I find?

How much information may I find?

How long might the search take?

Can I read it (handwriting, Old Scots, Latin)?

Beyond the Old Parish Register – Route Finding